1. Changing Direction

As I parked my new company car in the undercover parking allocated to me by the company, I became acutely aware that today was different from yesterday – more so than normal – because today was not only the first day of the month, and the financial year, but also the first day in my new position as a sales manager.

"Sales Manager", I heard myself saying aloud. Sounded good – no, great! In my excitement, I had hardly slept the previous night, going through my meticulously thought-out plan. Speaking of which, everything was going according to plan – well, actually, going ahead of plan. Here I was, only twenty-seven, a Business Science graduate, cum laude, but doing what I had always loved, selling – and always done (successfully, of course), since I first learned in Grade 3 that I could make extra pocket money if I sold the extra sandwich I had asked my mother to make, to the highest bidder. Little did she know...

And I had just completed my first formal job as the most successful sales representative my company had seen in its not so shabby history. After all, I had made its Master Class, an elitist international group of super performers, in just my first year. Of course, that was unheard of and some people in high places had wanted to prevent my entry into the club until later in my career but what could they do? I had more than fulfilled all the criteria – and then gone on to increase my sales figures in years 2, 3 and 4 by 23%, 25% and 34% (the recession notwithstanding) respectively, which more than justified the decision they couldn't avoid making. Top of the class, by the proverbial mile. The story of my life...

"Gee, how I love it when a plan comes together...earlier than planned!" I heard myself think, remembering that I had set myself five years for this promotion. "So, does that mean I should move National Sales Manager forward a year too?" Oh, well, plenty of time to think of that.

Getting out of the car, I ran through my plans for the day. I had eight reps now reporting to me – and wanted to double this number by the end of the financial year. I still felt uneasiness as I pondered again over my decision to meet with the team first thing but pushed this aside blaming the sense of apprehension mixed with adrenalin with which I normally faced new things. What was I going to cover with them again? Okay, the order was important. First, my vision. Then, our respective roles in achieving that vision. Finally, my expectations of them. "Well, here goes," I said as I entered the reception area, greeting everyone there in the process. Eight o'clock, on the dot!

The first thing that struck me as I walked through our area of the office was how quiet it was. There were two reasons for this: firstly, the team members were all huddled around the coffee machine at the far end of the room – and they seemed to have stopped talking when I walked in. With a naivety I was sure I didn't posses, I couldn't work out why. Secondly, only three of the team were present.

"Hi, Team," I called out trying to achieve a multitude of things at once, including breaking the silence, hiding my being put off by more than half the team being late, and trying to will the presence of the others. "We still on for quarter past?"

"Well, I am not sure, Tony," Liz, the most senior sales rep present responded. "George is stuck in traffic and Craig said he just had to drop off a product package at Dr Remington's rooms."

"What about Susan?" I found myself battling to hide my disappointment and frustration.

"No news from her so I assume she is on her way," responded Linda.

"I guess that's a pretty fine way to start," I said trying, unsuccessfully, I feared, really hard to make it sound light-hearted. "Well, could someone please call everyone and find out what time the whole team is likely to be here so we can convene the meeting for then?"

"Sure, we will each make some calls," Liz offered. "Tony, how long do you think the meeting will take? I also have an important meeting with a client set for 9.30."

Shooting the Lights Out
A Guide to Consistent Effective Management

A Story

by
Lauron Buys

"I wish I'd had a book like this when I was promoted from being the top sales consultant to being the National Sales Manager. The parable style makes it easy to read and to connect with. The tools are useful and so clearly explained that anyone could put them into practice.

In my view, this book will be extremely useful to all who have staff reporting to them, from supervisors and team leaders to senior managers."

Wendy van Elden
Previously National Sales Executive
Lexis Nexis SA
And now a professional Coach, Mentor & Trainer

"Lauron has really delivered in his latest book, *Shooting the Lights Out*. This book is gold for anyone in sales, sales management or people development. Lauron has written a book that is pure alchemy. He has managed to pen the secrets of human transformation, the likes of which I have never seen before. Lauron takes us on a journey of the transformation of a normal person just like you or me from salesperson to sales manager. In doing so, he shares the real experiences of a newly appointed sales manager, the problems we all face in this transition phase. Most importantly Lauron gives us the tools we need for the unification and development of a sales team and individual salespeople, serving a common purpose and achieving a common goal.

In this easy to read book, Lauron has unpacked what others have tried and failed to achieve. The tools are easy to understand and implement. Once you pick this little gem up, you will not put it down until the last page is done and he leaves you wanting more.... "

Roderick Ware
Regional Sales Manager
Momentum Financial Planning

"I think that the whole message is brilliant because it is a holistic approach to sales leadership as opposed to sales management and done in a very real and practical format."

Brian Findlay
Former Director, Nedbank Ltd

The best laid plans, I thought to myself, feeling them all come crumbling down. "Look, let's just try to get everyone here as soon as possible. I don't anticipate our meeting taking too long but if we are still busy and you need to go, so be it."

I went to my office, sat down, breathed deeply – a number of times – before taking my laptop out and booting up. Thirty seven emails, all since midday the previous day! Soon I was deeply engaged in my responses, one in particular. After what seemed a few minutes, I glanced at the time at the bottom right hand corner of my screen. Eight fifty! What had happened to the stragglers? Why had Liz and the others not come back to me? Rushing out into the open plan office I noticed that only a clerk was there, getting on with her work.

"Where is everyone?" I asked.

"Didn't you get the message?" she replied. "Liz emailed you about twenty minutes ago that they were ready and would wait for you in the Boardroom."

Probably the bored room by now, I thought. Gee, had I taken that long on my emails. Why hadn't I noticed her email come in? Anyway, better head off to the Boardroom and get going.

"Really sorry I kept you guys waiting but I didn't notice your email come in, Liz. Perhaps that's a good place to start," I said with a little but loud voice in my head shouting *no, no, stick to your agenda!* Seemingly powerless to stop myself I nevertheless continued. "Can we make a rule that we don't communicate with each other by email when we can just as easily communicate in person?" As they nodded, I had the distinct feeling that I had just created a millstone around my neck which would was sure to come back at me someday soon. At the same time, the voice in my head continued to remind me that I hadn't started the way I had planned. *You are going to be sorry. Just keep to the damn agenda.* Strange things happen in this role, I concluded.

"Well, we don't have much time so let's get on with the agenda. I thought we would talk, firstly, about how I see the team operating, kind of what I have in mind as our vision," I said, confusing the order, and myself a little in the process. *So much for preparing an agenda.* "I think we have a really good team here – all of you are pretty capable and competent. I see this as a time of growth. The economy seems to be coming out of the recession – not that I allowed that to get in my way in the past. As you know, this being the first day of the financial year, we have been set a team target that is 20% up on last year. I think we are capable of 30 and want to suggest that we make that our internal target. Okay?" *The agenda, Tony.* "For the foreseeable future, I am going to keep my customer list and continue to sell to them. I am confident that my figures will go up by at least 30%." *Once a sales person, always a sales person. Why prepare an agenda if you are just going to wing it anyway?*

"Will you have the time, now that you are sales manager too?" This time it was George, the most experienced rep there. George was in his late fifties and, I feared, had one and half eyes on his retirement.

"Yeah, thanks for raising that, George. Selling is in my blood – and I know that the company probably expects me to shed some of the sales load but I think they will understand when they see the numbers come in. Also, whilst I see us as a team, I believe you are, as I said, all capable salespeople. The last thing I want to do is to micromanage anyone. You are all captains of your own position, so to speak, so I want to...to..to like empower you. I would like to give you the freedom to express yourselves out there. Sure, I am here if you need me but for the rest I will be keeping an eye on all of our numbers – so, I suggest that is where you focus too. Okay!" *Congratulations, that's also sure to come back at you! You're throwing strategic boomerangs into every sentence.*

"But," George started, and then stopped.

"What, George?"

"No, it's okay. It's fine," he said, in retrospect, with a distinct lack of actual persuasiveness.

"Okay, I would like to have these meetings every second Friday so we can keep up with each other. So, please put that in your diaries now so that we don't have any repeats of this morning," I announced. "We're under 'general'. Anyone got anything they want to talk about?"

When I think about it now, it wasn't so much the silence that should have attracted my attention but the look on their faces. To this day, I can still see their faces clearly – in fact, more clearly than I ever saw it then: for them, Armageddon had arrived!

Fortunately for them, and me, the saviour of the world walked into my office just ten minutes later.

....

"Good morning, Tony, how are things going on your first day in the saddle?"

"Morning, Paulo. Fine, thank you," I replied, not really understanding why it hadn't sounded as convincing as I had intended.

"'Fine, thank you'", Paulo mimicked. "You don't sound so sure. What's up?"

Paulo was the National Sales Manager, my new boss, a wonderful person I just seemed to have got on with from the moment we had met on my first day in the office when he had almost burst into my area in an almost identical manner. The company had a policy as part of its induction programme in terms of which a senior manager was allocated to a new staff member for the first three months to ensure that they settled and learnt how things were done in the company. During that time I had built a huge amount of admiration for Paulo and had found him easy to talk to, even if he seemed to be reigning me in all the time – a process he had euphemistically and jokingly referred to as 'channelling your discretionary energy'! After the first three months he had stayed in touch on a more infrequent basis but I guess, of everyone at BCM Healthcare Suppliers, he was probably the person who knew me the best – and, as it worked out, whom I came to trust the most.

"Actually, Paulo, I am not sure why that came out like that. Things are really fine. I am in a great place at the moment. I had my first meeting with my team this morning and it went well, I thought, even if it didn't go quite as I planned."

"Tell me more about your meeting."

So I told him – probably in more detail than I had intended.

"Okay, I am hearing that there might be a couple of points about the meeting that you are not sure about. Are you able to put your finger on these?"

"Perhaps there are two things. Firstly, I have always got on really well with the team but there was a different vibe in the room today. I thought things would be more or less the same between us. Then, secondly, the mood seemed to change during the meeting."

"Would you like to explore these a little?" I nodded. "What do you think they were expecting this morning?"

"I am not sure what you mean."

"Well, your expectations seem to have been that the relationships you have with them would carry on in much the same way. If you were them, what would your expectations have been? Remember, if you are going to get into their shoes to answer this question, you have to take your own off first, so to speak – you need to look at it through their eyes, rather than your own."

"Gee, that's not easy. I guess they know me quite well. They've all been in the game longer than I have. I suppose they were as apprehensive as I was this morning – waiting to see what I was going to do."

"And what did they see when they looked at you before and in the meeting?"

"Umm, I am not sure. Perhaps they saw this cocky – actually, make that full-blown arrogant - youngster trying to take control of things and tell them how things were going to be done in future."

"And, if you were them, how would you have felt?"

"A little intimidated, and indignant, I guess. 'Yesterday he was the same as us and now he thinks he is better than us.' Something like that..."

"Okay. So, there would be some resistance. Let's hold that thought for a moment and go to your second concern. If you think back, when did the mood change in the room?"

"It seemed to be when George spoke." Paulo nodded to me to elaborate. "He seemed to be opposed to me retaining my clients. What he doesn't understand is that I have spent four years building up some really great relationships with my clients. What he also doesn't understand is that selling is in my blood." By now I was building up a head of steam.

"I can see you feel strongly about this. What role did you play in the change of mood in the room?"

"I suppose I was pretty dogmatic about my view."

"What impact do you think that would have had on you if you were a team member?"

"I guess I would have shut up too."

"That's interesting. So, what do you think the team needs from you now that you are their sales manager?"

"Gee, you ask some tough questions. I suppose they hope that I will keep bringing in big numbers, and leave them to their own devices – not get in their way; except of course if they ask for help."

"Is that how *you* see your new role too?"

"I guess so." Then, almost as an after-thought, because one thing I do well is catch on fast, "I think I see what you are getting at. You want to know what I would expect of the sales manager if I were them."

It was almost a question – and Paulo duly obliged. "Yes, perhaps it would help if you thought of it at two levels: what did you expect of Harry when he was your sales manager? And what do you think we expect of you in your new role?"

"The first one is easy – you were right: because I knew I was bringing more than the numbers required of me, I wanted to be left alone to get on with it, except when I needed some help. The second one is more difficult – help me out here."

"Okay, let me put it this way. Why would we give you promotion and great perks at considerable expense to the company if you were just going to do more of the same – bring in the numbers with perhaps the odd bit of help for your colleagues chucked in?"

"But I thought I got the promotion because I was the best rep."

"Yes, but do you think you would have got the new role if that was *all* we saw?"

"Whew, I guess I am a people's person and get on with the team members. I've also got a big mouth and am not scared to voice my opinion. Umm..."

"What kind of opinions do you hold about the team?"

"I guess the big one is that it should be a team but that currently we are a group of individuals. If we acted more like a team, then I am convinced that the numbers would get bigger."

"So your role in achieving this now that you are sales manager would be what?"

"Ensuring that we start becoming a team. If I am the team's leader, then I need to facilitate this – facilitate that we work together towards a common goal. Things like that. I guess I need to help the team and its individual members find ways to make the numbers. Gee, the management side is starting to sound like a full time job. I see what George might have been getting at – I will need to do less sales, not more."

"Less?"

"Oh no! You actually mean 'none', don't you? Gee, what about all the great relationships I have built over a long period of time? Do I just give those up now?"

"Would you be giving those relationships up? Or would the nature of your relationship with them just change?"

"But if I distributed my clients to the reps, then I wouldn't see my clients."

"You are right in the sense that you wouldn't necessarily see them in the same capacity as you have been seeing them up to now. But your relationship with these clients of the company are critical – so one of the challenges you have is to work out how you can retain a different level of relationship with them and other clients currently being serviced by the reps. Does that make sense?"

"Yeah, I guess it does in principle but I am going to have to give a little thought to the detail. I am sensing that my relationship with these clients now moves from a sales emphasis to kind of a marketing role. So, I might see them at functions we arrange, for example. In addition, I might see them too when I do joint visits with the reps – gee, I hadn't thought of that. In fact, there appears to be quite a lot I haven't thought of. I thought I would add that before you did!!"

"Not at all. On the contrary, I am really pleased to see that the pieces are starting to fall into place for you. The most important thing for many sales people to get when they move into management is that their role changes completely – they are not going to be doing more of the same. If it helps you, your role is still one of business development – but this time it is facilitating (and I would like to emphasise the word 'facilitating') the development of business by the reps. Whilst you were the rep with the best results, we believed that you were the person who could most successfully make this transition, effectively the transition from managing yourself to managing others. But, hey, I need to go to another meeting now. Have you found today useful?"

"Wow, my learning curve just went up a thousand percent. Is there any way we could do this again. I think it would really help me."

"Sure. I am really glad you found it useful. I suggest that we do this on a weekly basis and see how it goes. Is that okay with you?" I found myself nodding unwittingly and he went on. "What I think would also be useful for you would be for you to email me the answers to the following three questions: First, what are you going to stop doing in your new capacity? Second, what are you going to start doing? And lastly, what are you going to continue doing? How's that?"

"Great!" I said, thinking that this sounded easy enough. With that he got up, greeted me and was gone.

Armageddon had been averted. Well, not yet. I needed to do that email and then implement its contents. I turned to my laptop and found I had to think somewhat deeper than I had anticipated in order to answer the questions. After what seemed quite a while I typed the email to Paulo:

Stop	• Selling • Focusing on tasks
Start	• Focusing on people • Seeing yourself as others see you
Continue	• Holding conversations with • the team • team members

2. Acing our objectives
...instead of each other

This time it was me knocking on Paulo's door.

"Hi, Tony. Thank you for being on time. Take a seat; and I am going to come around, if you don't mind, and sit on this side of the desk with you," he said as he moved the other chair so that it was ninety degrees from mine.

"That's interesting," I remarked.

"What is?"

"It is the first time I have noticed anyone coming around to this side of the desk."

"Why do you think I did that?"

"I dunno. It certainly has a symbolic gesture about it, your coming to my side of your desk, your coming to me."

"Yes, there certainly is a bit of that. For me, the desk itself is a symbol, a symbol of power – so that when it is between us, our hierarchical difference is emphasised. It becomes my home game, if you like, and your away game – the very opposite of what my purpose is in these conversations. In this space, we need to have equal status otherwise the contributions are unequal."

"But you are my boss, so your status is higher than mine," I said thinking I was stating the obvious.

"Is that what you felt in our conversation last week?"

"I didn't think about it...which means I was quite comfortable...okay, so I am starting to get what you mean but I can't quite put it into words."

"Can you think of a metaphor that might describe what you are trying to say?"

"Come to think of it, yes. When we are on opposite sides of the desk, it can seem adversarial – so, in a heavy conversation it might seem as if we are playing tennis against each other. On the other hand, when we are on the same side of the net or desk, it is like we are playing doubles."

"I like that. Great. Do you think there is any difference in what the conversation sounds like as a result?"

"I guess the tone changes. The partners on the same side of the net are working together, collaborating, against the opposition on the other side of the net. The tone would be completely different if they were on opposite sides of the net trying to win points off each other."

"Your metaphor is really working for me. So, if we are playing doubles together on one side of the net, what is on the other side of the net?"

"Wow, that's not easy. I guess all it could be is our objectives. Yes, we would be playing together to achieve our objectives – and those objectives are on the other side of the net. Does that sound right?"

Paulo smiled. "The metaphor has really worked for me too," I continued. I like the notion of working with my team members, making sure I work *with* them, to achieve the goals on the other side of the net. It seems to me that that is a completely different approach to managing than the one I have always had in mind – it is far more...umm, facilitative, enabling. You are *helping* them to achieve what's required. Gee, that sounds pretty profound for me. Let me make a note of it before I forget it."

On my pad I wrote the following words and put a block around them so that they would stand out:

Play doubles tennis with my team

- play from the same side of the net
- play together to achieve the objectives on the other side of the net

"It is!" Paulo continued. "In fact, it is a really important point you are making and one that really complements what I would like us to consider discussing today. But before we do that, I would really like to hear how your week has gone since our last discussion."

"Yeah, it's been rather a busy week. I have met with each of the team members and told them that I am going to allocate all my clients to them. I had made up a schedule for each one of them. I had allocated each client to team members on the basis of criteria like my perception of their experience and ability and the importance of the client to the company. It was interesting because as it worked out they each got about the same amount of new business from these clients on last year's sales."

"What was their response?"

"Surprise was the most obvious response. There was a little scepticism as well. Some of them asked me why I was doing this, so I said that I wanted to focus my attention on helping them to get the numbers; that although the relationships belonged to them and they were accountable for those clients, I would continue to have a relationship with those clients; and that I hoped to build a relationship with all their clients as well, especially the most significant clients, so that I could assist them in that way to reach their figures. I don't think they could believe their ears, and for some of them I had to explain exactly what this meant so that they didn't think I would be in their way all the time. I think they are prepared to give it a try although they may be a little protective of their clients. In that sense, I think we might be battling to get onto the same side of our metaphorical net."

"What do you think that is about?"

"I guess if I was them I would also be a little reticent – I would like to see what this new young upstart has in him before I commit to him completely."

"What do you think this means you have to do before they will commit completely?"

"Probably build their trust – which sounds a big ask! They are all older and more experienced than me."

"But nowhere in what you have said to me, have I sensed that there is any real animosity – have I missed something?"

"No, you are right. As I say, they seem to be giving me a honeymoon period. But how do I build that trust?"

"What do you think the critical factors are for people to trust each other?"

"I don't know if I am going to get the order right or even think of everything but I guess when people genuinely care about how I am doing that is a big tick in the box. Also, they shouldn't act in any way that makes me think they are untrustworthy...they need to walk the talk, I suppose."

"How might you show that you care?"

"I suppose by taking an interest in them – how they are, how they are doing."

"That interest in them would have to be genuine, right? How would you show them that it is genuine interest?"

"I would have to actually be interested in them as people, not just go through the motions."

"Yes, I think that's right. So you would ask questions that show you are interested. But I think it is more than this. What do you think might be the most important way to show that you are actually interested in them as people?"

I thought for a moment before it came to me. "I know – to really listen to their answer, without interrupting, without letting my own thoughts get in the way; to really listen to what *they* have to say."

"Yes, that seems absolutely crucial to me. I think that people feel valued when they are listened to. It's probably the biggest compliment we can pay them because we are saying, 'what you are saying is valuable'. Okay, so the criteria we have so far are:

Building mutual trust

- Genuinely care
- Listen
- Act trustworthily
- Walk the talk

If you did those four things, do you think you would build their trust?"

"Sure, but isn't trust a two-way thing?"

"Yes, it is most certainly mutual when you get it right. But whose responsibility do you think it is in this case to build trust?"

"When you put it like that it becomes obvious, doesn't it. Okay, thanks, I get it."

"Okay, I would like to leave you with something that you might like to mull over and comment about when we meet next week. Is that okay?"

"You make it sound like you have given me nothing else to think about! Just joking – but I am finding these meetings with you incredibly thought-provoking and I really appreciate the time you are giving me. I know you are very busy."

"It's a pleasure, Tony. But really, I am just doing my job. What do you think my job is?"

"I had always assumed that it was to make sure that your sales managers hit the numbers. Something tells me, however, that that is only a part of it."

"Correct. I believe that is the consequence of what I do in my role – in other words, the output rather than the input, but I am sure we will come back to that. But it does lead me into the model I wanted to share with you to mull over, so let me get into it right away. Would you agree that, in the workplace, the following are inter-related: performance, learning and satisfaction or job fulfillment?"

"Yeah, I can see that."

"Okay, if that is the case," Paulo was drawing on a piece of paper lying between us, "then we can join them with a triangle like this, not so?"

Performance

Learning   Satisfaction

He continued. "I'm a little outspoken on this but I really believe we need to heed the message I hope I leave with you in this concept. It's not mine; I got it from a book I once read called *The Inner Game of Work* by a guy Timothy Gallwey[1]. Anyway, let me get on with the idea. I want you to tell me how much emphasis most organisations, including our own, put on Performance. I am going to put my pen near the Performance apex and move it upwards until you tell me to stop."

I liked this game and waited until his pen was well out of the triangle and above the word "Performance" before saying (with a huge smile on my face), "Okay, you can stop now."

"You're right. I have asked several people to do the exercise, even my mates in other organisations, and everyone does the same thing – it appears that all organisations put an inordinate amount of emphasis on performance. What we don't realise," he said, drawing once again, "is the impact this emphasis has. See if you agree."

Performance

Learning   Satisfaction

"Yeah, I see that. Makes sense, doesn't it. We put so much emphasis on performance that learning and satisfaction are adversely affected. But, we have to emphasise performance, don't we? If we didn't, we wouldn't hit our targets."

"Let me put it to you this way: does the level of emphasis we put on performance match the results we get? In other words, for every bit of emphasis we put on performance, do we get more actual performance? So, if we just keep

---

[1] Timothy Gallwey: The Inner Game of Work (2000): 85-86

increasing the amount of emphasis, will actual performance levels just keep increasing at the same rate, forever, ad infinitum?"

"When you put it like that, the answer is definitely 'no'. So, I guess what you are saying is that at some stage we become less effective, ultimately ineffective, with this approach. In fact, you're probably asking whether we might have gone past that point – will we in fact know when we have?"

"You catch on fast. Now you know why we made you sales manager." His big smile seemed to show he really enjoyed his joke. "But, if the three factors are inter-related as we initially said, what do we know?"

"I guess that any over-emphasis of one leads to a lack in the others. So, that would mean that we need to place equal emphasis on each."

"And what would the impact of that be?"

"An increase in actual performance, actual learning and actual satisfaction, I guess."

"Bingo."

"So, how do we use this information, in practical terms? What should I actually do with my team to ensure this happens?"

"That's what I thought you might like to mull over and discuss next time."

3. **A Question of Learning trumping Teaching**

"I must be having fun," I said to Paulo as I sat down.

"Why's that?" he enquired.

"Well, it's just like yesterday that we had the last session. Time flies when you are having fun."

"'Session'?" his eyebrows rose. "Makes it sound like therapy! That's certainly not my intention."

"Sorry, must have been a Freudian slip, if you'll excuse the pun – I don't know why I said it; it's not a term I use much. But, actually, it's not inaccurate. For me, these are far more than meetings or appointments that we have. I guess, I guess, for me, they are learning sessions."

"That's nice to hear," Paulo commented, his eyebrows now back to their default setting.

"Can I ask you a question?" It was my turn to enquire.

"Sure," came the inevitable reply.

"On Tuesday, when I bumped into you in the corridor. You did something I've never experienced before in my short career."

"What's that?"

"You made reference to our discussion in these sessions."

"Oh," he smiled, "and why is that strange?"

"Not strange, but unusual. In my four years here I have had three and a half bosses. Otto doesn't count because he left after my first two months."

"I wouldn't take it personally." Clearly Paulo was in a really good mood. "So, what's so unusual?"

"Well, firstly, they hardly ever had one-on-ones with me. But, more importantly, they never referred to our previous discussions outside of the meeting room – in fact, that means they probably never referred back to our previous discussions. Not even to things that might have been said in the occasional team meetings. It was as if those kinds of things were only discussed behind closed doors."

"That's interesting. What makes this important to you?"

"I suppose it is the lack of continuity it creates. It also minimises, in my mind anyway, the importance of those sessions. I mean, if what was said was, like, really important, then another reference to it would reinforce that fact. Not to refer to it kind of says 'that was important then, other stuff is important now'. We have had two sessions – there's that word again – and although we have spoken about different things, it is almost as if it is a continuous conversation. And then when we met in the corridor and you asked me how the mulling was going, well, it added continuity and, in a nice relaxed way, said what I was mulling over was important – in fact, not only that the mulling over was important but that our conversations were important. I have just had another thought – it told me that these conversations are not only important to me, but they are important to you too! And that makes me feel valued. Wow, I never thought about things like this before."

"The issue of being valued came up in our last discussion..."

"Yeah, when we talked of building trust. Sorry, I interrupted you."

"No, that's okay. That is what I was going to say. I'd like to know how the trust building is going in a moment but let's finish this part of the conversation first. So, you said you had a question for me?"

"Oh, yes. In fact, I think it's grown to two – it's called inflationary conversations." It was my turn to be creatively flippant. "Firstly, did you intentionally link back to our last session's conversation when we met in the corridor? And, if so, why?"

"Well, the answer to your first question is 'yes'. The answer to your second is a little longer. The easy answer is that I see every conversation with my people as an opportunity for us both to learn. Last time we spoke of the three factors in what Tim Gallwey called The Work Triangle, namely performance, learning and satisfaction. Remember, the three are inter-related. Accordingly, if every conversation is an opportunity to learn, then every conversation will impact on performance. The way I see it, we have formal performance conversations twice a year when we have our appraisals. In between we have fairly formal monthly team meetings and regular, in our case, weekly, even less formal one-on-one, err, sessions. The corridor 'sessions' provide further informal opportunities to continue the conversation, thereby increasing the focus and momentum of the conversations and, therefore, the learning. I think they provide the reinforcement you mentioned."

"Sort of the glue that holds them all together. And if we learn as we go and this learning is focused, performance will be impacted positively, and we will have more fun in our jobs."

"Yes, that's more or less how I see the theory working. But there is another important element to it and that relates to the learning we experience in our conversations. In an earlier conversation, you indicated that you were learning so much from these conversations – why do you think that is?"

"You just make me think so differently about all the stuff we talk about. In just a couple of weeks I reckon I am a different person, especially with my team."

"What about our conversations gets you to think?"

"I guess it's what you have just done – it's the questions you ask. I wanted to ask you why you do that?"

"Well, if I answered your queries by telling you my views, who would be doing the thinking?"

"You have just done it again, asked a question." So, my smart-assed approach was still alive and well, despite our conversations! Almost to cover up, I continued, "You would be doing the thinking. And I would be doing the learning, wouldn't I?"

"Well, let's test that. In the past, let's say with your teachers at school and your three and a half bosses over the last four years, just how much of what they told or suggested to you or advised you to do, did you accept and apply? Give me a rough percentage."

"Now you've got me. I think I am quite a maverick and I seem to check stuff before I just accept it. If I had to say, it would be 20 to 30 percent...on good days! That sounds disrespectful, almost irreverent. " I found myself chuckling at my arrogance. "But I am sure that I am not the norm?"

Paulo saw through my thinly veiled, slightly desperate, attempt to be normal. "In fact, you *are* pretty normal. In my experience, most people take some of what is told to them – that part that sits comfortably with them – but they chuck a lot. So, my theory continues that if most people I have checked with are like that, and I am certainly like that, then the people who are in my team, mostly selected by me, are probably like that, so wouldn't I be insulting them by thinking I have all the answers, and that they are simply going to absorb and apply everything I have to say? And what good would it do if they are going to chuck a quarter of what I say anyway – as you say, on good days. I guess it amounts to: What is the good of my trying to teach people if they only learn a little from what I teach? It's far better, according to my logic, to find ways to help them learn. After all, I certainly don't have all the answers, and even where I do have answers, who is to say they don't have better ones. In fact, I try to select people who I hope will often have answers, otherwise their value-add to the organisation is likely to be limited."

"It is starting to make a whole lot of sense to me."

"So, who does the thinking?'"

"I guess it is the person who is asked to answer."

"That's certainly true. In fact, perhaps my primary function as a manager is to help the people in my team think. If I do that, they will soon be able to resolve more and more complex challenges. But in order to ask a question that makes you think, I also need to think. The better the question, the better the learning. So, we both get to think a lot more deeply about the challenges we face. That's how we begin to extend all three corners of the Work Triangle beyond what we might think is possible. And besides, it means people can get on with it even if I am not in the office."

"Wow, that's powerful. I would really like to do that with my team but I am not sure where to start. I mean how do I know what question to ask?"

"My view is that it is a case of practice makes perfect. I mean, think about how you conduct your conversations now. How do you know what to say? If you take time to think about what the purpose of the conversation is and what you need to say, and then reflect afterwards on how that went, well, you are going to get better and better. But if I could give you one tip, it would be this: the better you listen, the better your questions will become. Use what you hear the other person say; the question is there, not in your head. It's not everything but it will take you a long, long way to asking good questions. Trust yourself. How does that sound to you?"

"I think I get that, although I think it is going to take a lot of practice. I find myself thinking of what my next question is going to be or what I want to say, rather than listening fully."

"When you are doing that, you are listening to respond. The most important purpose of listening, though, is to understand, not to respond. So instead of listening to respond, focus on listening for understanding."

"Wow, you make that sound so simple. I guess it comes back to practice. Can I ask you another question? We've been talking about moving from teaching or telling to helping to listening and for the first time I have noticed that you haven't stuck only to questions – sometimes you have given me your views and answers. How do you know when to do what?

"That comes with practice too. But I have a couple of ground rules I try to stick to. The first is that I aspire to be what is called non-directive (where I ask questions) 80 percent of the time. It is a pretty stretching target, one that I seldom achieve, but I hold it out in front of me all the time. Generally, the closer I get the more learning seems to be achieved. But there are times when doing so is impractical – for example, sometimes technical or basic knowledge would take too long to get through if I did it non-directively so it just doesn't make sense to spend hours on it. But I try to be quite disciplined about getting back into non-directive mode as soon as that basic knowledge is in place."

"So, you keep tabs on just how much of the 20 percent you are using up? That makes sense."

"There is another way of looking at it as well." He got up to draw an arrow on the white board in his office. "Would you agree, after the conversations we have had, that the more one asks questions – the more we stay on the right-hand side of this arrow - so the more empowering it is, the more people learn, and the more effective we are as managers?" I nodded. "And, conversely, the more we tell what and how – that is, the more we are on the left-hand side of the arrow – the more controlling we are being, the less our people are learning and, by definition then, the less effective we are as managers?"

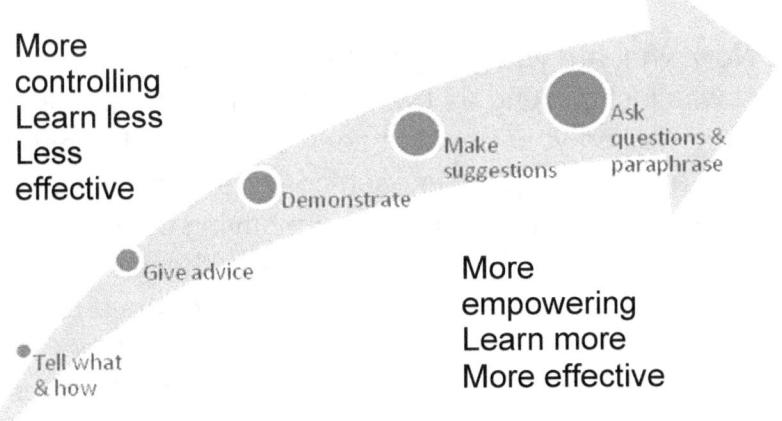

More
controlling
Learn less
Less
effective

Demonstrate

Give advice

Tell what
& how

Make
suggestions

Ask
questions &
paraphrase

More
empowering
Learn more
More effective

"Yeah, that makes sense too."

"For me, there is one more really important point I want to make here to reinforce what I am saying. If that is the case," he said pointing to the arrow, "and let us say that in the conversation I am having with you, I am asking questions and paraphrasing – that is, I am on the empowering and learning side of the arrow – and then I make a suggestion, what has happened by definition?"

"I guess you have become one step more controlling, I am going to learn a little less, and so you are just that little less effective."

"That's it. So, I believe we have to be acutely aware that this is what is happening - every time we move to the left on this conversational level, we are becoming more controlling, the people learn less, and *we* are less effective. Is that helpful?"

"It certainly drives it home."

"We seem to have used up most of our time and I haven't had an opportunity to find out how the 'mulling' went?"

"I spent a lot of time thinking about what we did last week but, gee, our discussion today has taken it all to a completely new level."

"Okay, then let's sum up. What are the most important things that you will take out of today's conversation? If it helps you, you can write it up on the white board."

"Let me see," I said getting up and walking across the room. I paused for a moment and then started writing down some notes.

"Good. Now what are you going to do with that list?"

"I know. I was just thinking as I was writing the list that this is all good and well on your board. It seems to me that I need to consciously apply each point in each conversation I have with my team members. At the moment, I am having conversations with them but, in terms of what we have said, these conversations tend to be on the left-hand side of the arrow and there are also lots of conversations, especially if they are not pre-arranged, where I don't take the opportunity to focus on performance, learning and fulfilment. I guess the point is that these conversations are not add-ons in terms of my job function. I am having them anyway, or I should be having them. It's more about this..." I said moving back to the white board and adding the heading so that the note now read:

Holding the same conversations more effectively

- Every conversation is an opportunity to improve
  - performance
  - learning and
  - fulfilment
- People learn more when they are made to think
- My job is to help people to learn through helping them to think
- I am more effective when I stay on the right-hand side of the arrow
- To ask better questions, LISTEN FOR UNDERSTANDING

4. Managing results makes managing difficult

"So, how's your week been?" asked Paulo, ushering me into his office.

"Great, thanks. Yeah, it seems to be coming together in many ways. In others, I am not so sure."

"Okay, so what has been working for you?"

"I think the notion that every conversation is an opportunity to help my team members learn, improve their performance and find fulfilment has been incredible for me. It has changed my whole approach. I am looking out for more opportunities to chat to them. I am looking for things I can help them with rather than trying to catch them out. And I am finding – and I think they are too – that I am able to help them, despite my age and relative inexperience; I think they are as surprised by what they are experiencing as I am. I think they experience it as my really caring – and I am, far more than I thought I was capable of. I find I *do* care. As a result, I think the trust levels on both sides are growing steadily."

"You sound very pleased with yourself."

"More with the way we, as a team, are gelling. I think we are succeeding in playing doubles tennis, but the quality of the tennis isn't great yet."

"What in particular isn't working for you?"

"Two things come to mind immediately: firstly, I am still not comfortable with my questioning ability and, secondly, I often feel as if I am running out of things to talk about. Come to think of it, the two things might be related."

"Could be. Tell me more about your discomfort in terms of asking questions."

"Well, I tried to do the listening thing as we discussed but I just seem to have so much traffic in my head that when it comes to my turn to say something, there's a complete snarl-up and I don't know what to ask."

"Let me see if I understand you correctly. What I hear you saying is that you just have so many thoughts going on in your head that you don't know which one to use?" When I nodded, he went on. "Last time we briefly mentioned the primary purpose of listening – can you remember what that is?"

"Yes, to understand what the speaker is saying. We talked about listening for understanding and not listening to respond. And I get that – but I don't seem to know what to do with it."

"Okay, so the purpose of listening from the perspective of the listener is listening for understanding. But what if we looked at it from the perspective of the speaker: for them, what do they need the listener to do to make them feel they have been heard and understood?"

"I suppose the listener needs to acknowledge in some way that he understands."

"Correct again. So, perhaps a critical aspect of listening is for the speaker to know that they have been heard and understood by the listener. How could the listener achieve this?"

"I guess it wouldn't be enough for them to say they understand because the speaker wouldn't know whether that was true or not. Umm, maybe the listener needs to check his understanding...perhaps by summarising what they have just heard...or, umm, by asking the speaker to clarify what they mean where they, the listener, aren't sure."

"Good, by summarising or clarifying the speaker will know whether he or she is being understood and heard. What needs to happen for the listener to be listening at that level?"

"The listener needs to make sure there are no distractions, look the speaker in the eye and engage with them."

"Correct, but I have found that I can do all the physical things to avoid distractions – shut down my computer, close the door, switch off my cell phone, take my landline off the hook – as well as seemingly engage with the speaker quite convincingly but not be there for them. I can be quite convincing even while I am considering what I will be doing on the weekend, or in the next meeting. That ever happened to you?"

"Absolutely. So what is the solution?"

"I think we have to be present – we have to be in both the here and the now – when we are listening at this level. You spoke earlier about stuff going on in your head which I suppose meant you weren't in the communal now (if there is such a thing); you were listening in your head, instead of the speaker's. Does that make sense?"

"Yes. And that is what you mean by being present. I suppose the way to do that is, as you said, by being able to summarise what they are saying."

"That's right. The first question that you sit with when you are listening at this level is: 'What are they saying?'"

"You mean there are other questions?"

"Yes, there is one more. Because when we are dealing with people at this level, we need more information so that we might have greater insight into what is going on for them and what they might need. Any idea of what the question might be?"

"I don't know but I will have a flyer. Maybe another question is what do they feel about what they are saying?"

"Gee, didn't expect you to get that. You're not a mind-reader, are you? Yes, the second one is: How do they feel about what they are saying? Can you see that answering this question will provide greater insight?"

"I never thought of that, but yes."

"Okay, would you like to summarise what you are going to practise when you are listening to your team members?"

"Yes, that would be helpful. Do you mind if I use the board again?" Paulo nodded and I walked across to the white board and wrote:

Listening for understanding

- Be present
- Ask self
  - "What are they saying?"
  - "How do they feel about what they are saying?"

"Great. Let's move onto your second concern: if I recall it was what should your questions be about? In practical terms, are you asking what the content of your conversations should be about?"

"Yes, but to be more specific, what do we talk about after we have dealt with the numbers?"

"Can you give me an example?"

"Yes, I was having a session with Craig yesterday and I showed him his numbers for last month. We agreed that he would need to do better this month and he agreed that he would. That was it. End of discussion – three and a half minutes! I just didn't feel it was effective."

"I think I see what you mean. Before we begin, and as an aside, we sometimes feel that these conversations need to be substantial in terms of length to be effective. Remember, the corridor coaching we discussed last time: quantity does not necessarily equal quality; effectiveness equals quality. I know you know that but I thought I would just reinforce that. Okay? Then, when we talk about numbers we would be talking about the performance factor on the work triangle, right?"

"Right."

"As a heads-up, let me give you a formula you might find useful", he said walking across to the ever-useful white board:

$$Performance = Potential - Interference$$

[2]

"P=P-I, for short," he continued. "'Performance', in this case with Craig, would be your reference to the numbers. Craig has a sales role. If you think of sales as a process, with inputs, throughputs and outputs, what part of the process do the numbers fall into?"

"Must be outputs."

"Correct. Many, if not most, managers fall into the trap of managing outputs only but if we look at the formula on the board, there are two other factors we could include in our performance conversations with our team members. By the way, your example of Craig illustrates another point: he didn't make target last month. Is that the only time we as managers should be talking performance with our team members? In other words, do we manage performance only when there is under-performance?"

"I think I had assumed that was the case until this moment but I suppose there is nothing stopping us having conversations with team members who are performing."

"Like our conversations?"

"Now that you mention it, yes."

---

[2] Myles Downey: Effective Coaching (2003): 10-12

"Yes, as I see it, our role as manager is primarily about improving performance and developing all our people. Performance management, despite the way it is usually used, does not necessarily equal under-performance management; it is what it says, the management of performance, whether under- or over-, and for all members of our team. That is our primary function as managers. Moving onto the next factor in the formula, what are the various ways we might define 'potential'?"

"The first thing that comes to mind is someone's innate potential in an area. So someone is, for example, a natural sales person or they might not be. In this sense, it seems to be related to talent. But it seems to me, if I look at the formula, that it is a little wider than pure talent, and fulfilling that talent. From a manager's perspective, in the sense of managing the performance of someone, it is probably more about our ability to help someone reach their potential, our ability to help them to be at the top of their game."

"Good. So, what are the wider factors beyond mere talent that you would look at?"

"I suppose they could be training...could be product training and/or skills training, if they are short on these; or honing their skills in these areas. Okay, they are inputs or throughputs."

"And if you look at the formula, what happens if you increase potential by helping someone to be at the top of their game in this way?"

"Their performance goes up."

"That's right. And what do you think 'interference' might refer to?"

"It sounds like obstacles that are in the way of, in our case, the sales. Perhaps lack of stock or the delivery van is broken down."

"Those could well be examples of external interference. What is your role as sales manager in those circumstances?"

"To remove the obstacles?"

"Yes, you would remove the obstacle if it fell outside of the sales rep's area of influence. What if it was within their area of influence?"

"Well, then I suppose our job is to *help* them remove the obstacle."

"Yep. Up until now, we have probably been focusing on external obstacles. If those are examples of external interference, what might internal interference look like?"

"That's a tough one but let me try to work it out. It seems to me that the interference must be 'external' and 'internal' with reference to something. Could it be the company? No, don't think so. Oh, I know, it must be the person that we are applying the formula to – if I can put it like that. If it is internal to the person, then I guess it must be mental rather than physical. Like, umm, self-belief – or lack of it."

"Very good. Very good. Mental and emotional. Self-limiting and self-sabotaging beliefs are certainly examples of internal interference. Other examples might be things like fear, doubt, anxiety, procrastinating, catastrophising, complaining, or avoidance. So if we are able to reduce these for our sales people, then we are able to increase...?"

"Their performance – and so if we increase their potential *and* reduce their interference, we get a double whammy in terms of their performance. That's great. That gives me a lot to work on in the conversations. Thank you."

"I know it is quite a lot to take in today but I would like to stretch you a little further. Is that okay with you?"

He knew I just couldn't, and wouldn't, resist a challenge.

"Always!" came my semi-automatic response.

"Okay, let's go back to the idea of sales as a process. Once again, by definition all sales processes are just that – processes - and what we are going to work through now should apply in all industries and with all products. Okay, earlier we established that a process consists of inputs, throughputs and outputs. If we look at a sales process – and let's generalise it rather than make it specific to ours (we can do that later if we need to) – what do you think the inputs might be?"

"I would think that they would deal with things like choice of salesperson – selection, if you like. Training, I guess, would be another – both product training and sales skills training. Yeah, I think that probably covers the input side."

"Yes, and if we consider our P=P-I formula we discussed earlier, where would these inputs fit in?"

"If we think of it in terms of selection and product or sales skill training, these all should impact favourably on the potential of the person. With proper selection and training, the potential should be increased."

"I see it that way too. And what do you think throughputs consist of?"

"I guess that consists largely of the content of the sales skills and product training: things like prospecting, qualifying prospects, calling on prospects, needs analysis, choice of products to fulfil the needs, objections, closing sales etc. Did I leave anything out?"

"That doesn't matter for now – you have got the gist of it. If you think of our P=P-I formula, what might these steps of the process relate to?"

"Uhh, potential as well. They are all things one could increase in order to help someone to be at the top of their game."

"That's right. I like to use the term 'variables' to remind me that they are not constants and therefore that I can help people change the way they carry out or implement a variable so that they maximise their performance. All processes are made up of a sequence of variables, each of which we can impact in some way."

"Gee, that's helpful. It makes so much sense to look at it that way."

"Yes, but have a look at the process you have talked about in terms of both inputs and throughputs – those are all external inputs and throughputs, aren't they? Can you see that interference might fit in as an internal variable, probably mostly under throughputs."

"Okay, okay, yes, the penny is dropping. Could I summarise it diagrammatically so that I can see if I have got it right?"

"Of course. Help yourself."

I went to the white board and drew a block arrow. I knew that if sales was a process, it had to have an arrow somewhere. I divided the arrow into three parts: inputs, throughputs and outputs – the rest just seemed to fall into place.

Inputs (Potential)	Throughputs (Interference)	Outputs (Performance)
•Selection	•External variables (Potential)	•The numbers
•Training	•Lead generation process	•The service
•products	•Lead conversion process	•The relationship
•sales	•Inernal variables	

"This way, the outputs seem to become a natural consequence of the extent to which we effectively manage all the variables in the inputs and throughputs," I concluded.

"Exactly. We have been going for just over half an hour. Have we given you something to work on in terms of the content of your conversations? Or would you like to unpack how you might use this in an actual conversation with one of your team members."

"No, thanks a lot. I think I know how I am going to use this information. If you don't mind, I would like to try and work it out for myself and try it out – and, then, if I have any hiccups perhaps we can deal with them in the next session, if that's okay. Thanks, Paulo, that was great – lots to think about...and apply!"

"No problem. You seem to have understood the concepts pretty well so I am glad you have the confidence to try it. Let me know if you get stuck when you think it through in preparation. Otherwise, good luck, and I will see you next week, if I don't see you in the corridor before that!" We both chuckled. This was fun.

....

As I was due to see Liz an hour later, I decided I would try to apply my freshly-learned knowledge. After all, they say – quite who 'they' is, I don't know – but they say that knowledge is worth nothing unless and until it is applied.

In preparation for the meeting, I thought I would try to simplify what I had learned. I would focus on three things: listening for understanding, listening for how she felt about what she was saying, and fitting this all into the sales process framework.

After the earlier discussion with Paulo when we discussed the symbolism around the boss' desk, I had bought a round table with four chairs for my office and made a point of meeting my team members around that table. In fact, I had swapped my rather large desk for a smaller table, and taken away the visitor's chairs on the other side of it, to try to make the point that it was my working surface and that all meetings would happen around the round table. I hoped that would go some way towards neutralising any home ground advantage I might have.

Liz, punctual as always, knocked on my door on the dot of ten.

"Come in, Liz," I said, immediately rising from my table and moving towards the meeting table. I waited for her to take a seat so that I could take the one next to her, merely because I felt sitting opposite her felt quite adversarial for me, especially with the table between us. Sitting next to her, we were at ninety degrees and I reduced that even more by turning my chair slightly towards her, at the same time making sure that I didn't encroach on her space and looking to see if I could see any signs of discomfort or anxiety in her body language. None that I could detect anyway.

"How are things with you, Liz?" I asked trying to break the ice.

"Fine, thank you. Missing a bit of sleep, mind you, as my daughter is teething."

"I guess that privilege all lies before me." My wife was due in about three months. "It can't be pleasant having to go through one's children's challenges."

"No, but somehow we – and our children – get through it relatively unscathed."

"How is Jacob getting on in his first couple of weeks at school? Settling down?" I enquired remembering an exercise I had done earlier in the week for each of my team members:

Team member's name	All I know about them...	How I might be able to support them...

I had worked out that if I collated everything I knew about each of my team members and thought about how I could support them in their personal and work circumstances, I was more likely to build trust as well as find ways to get the most out of them. This was test time: testing 1, 2, 3...

"Gee, I didn't think you would remember a detail like that. Thank you, Tony. No, he is fine, loving it. They grow up so quickly."

"I see your sales are also growing quite quickly." I said without thinking and then realised that I was building on what she had just said. Ah! Perhaps the listening was starting to work after all. "You are on track. Would you like to take me through the numbers?" In my relatively brief sojourn as a sales representative, I had found it incredibly boring when my sales manager laboriously went through my numbers for me. I should know them better than anyone – after all, they were my sales, my business; and they are the most important reflection of what a sales representative does. Now, as a sales manager, my rationale went a little further: as well as being the sales representative's responsibility, it was an opportunity for them to be proud of what they did and to raise their successes and their challenges. Of course, I wasn't absolutely sure that this new-found theory of mine would work, but how else would I find out if my theories worked or not, if I didn't experiment with them!

For five minutes, Liz took me through her numbers with pride and...well, it seemed she felt motivated by what she was saying.

I summarised what she had said and then checked with her how she felt about giving me the feedback on her progress rather than the other way around. "It's different," she confided. "In the beginning, I was a little thrown but I seemed to warm to the task pretty quickly and found myself being quite proud of my achievements and, then, this in turn made me feel...well, quite motivated to keep up the good work."

Eureka, listening for understanding works, I found myself thinking, almost aloud. It was all the confirmation I needed.

"You have every right to feel proud of your achievements. I was wondering whether you would like to explore ways in which you might stretch yourself even further. We might as well do something with that extra energy you built up in the feedback." I smiled.

Her whole expression and manner changed. "Okay, but I don't know how many more hours I can put into the day. I think I am working flat out," she murmured defensively.

Whoops, Complacent Tony was back! I had stepped over a line I didn't see. Damage control time.

"I am really sorry, Liz. I honestly didn't mean it that way. I genuinely meant let's explore some stuff and see where it leads. I don't want you working any harder – it will just impact on your family time and I don't want that. If I am able to help you to explore various avenues, I thought, maybe we could find smarter ways for you to achieve, so that you don't have to work any extra hours. As we sit here, I honestly don't know what I mean in terms of outcomes of a discussion like this – I don't know what the answer is, or even if there are any answers. I merely thought the exploration might be interesting and, hopefully, worthwhile."

"I'm sorry too, Tony. I got a little defensive and perhaps over-reacted. Think it's the sleepless nights. The one thing I know about you is that you have good intentions – so I was out of line too. Let's do it."

"Are you sure this is a good time? Would you rather do it when you are more rested?" Part of me was in sincere damage control mode, with another part really amazed at the level of the conversation - Liz and I had never said much to each other before my promotion and now we were operating at a comfortably deep level.

"No, I am fine, thank you. Happy to explore."

"Okay. In this conversation, I would like to do something different. I want to get away from discussing results. After all, results are merely consequences of actions that go before. So," I said, putting a much neater diagram of the sales process than the one probably still on Paulo's board, in front of her, pointing to the relevant parts; "can we look at the sales process from a different angle to what we normally have in mind and explore this area, the throughputs? What do you see as the variables that you have control over in terms of lead generation? By controllable variables, I probably mean actions that you are able to decide whether you can change or not."

"Let me see...lead generation. You know what? I haven't thought of what I can do in that area for a very long time. I mean we have all become dependent on the marketing and advertising done by Marketing to surface new leads, on the one hand, and then on the other I – and I don't think I am alone – rely on our existing clients. Our products have been so good, we seem to hit our targets – and they get steeper every year, as you know – without fishing any wider. This exploratory game of yours is not bad, huh!"

"Seems like it might be better than I anticipated," I responded, knowing full well that the glow I felt inside was shining all over my face too. "Would it help you if we spent a little time brainstorming different ways in which you might be able to generate leads?"

Of course she agreed and we spent five minutes exploring different ideas, both possible and improbable, real and hypothetical. I had also been careful not to allow any justification of or judgment on any of them to take place during the brainstorming part of the session since I was scared that we would get distracted and lose brainstorming momentum. Discussion could take place later, if necessary. In the end we numbered them on the white board I had recently purchased, not in any order but merely to be able to make identification easier.

"So, are there any criteria you would like to apply in deciding which options you would like to try?" I asked when we were satisfied that the fourteen on the board probably formed an exhaustive list, for now anyway.

"I think I would like to pick the two or three options that are likely to give me the biggest returns in terms of leads in the shortest possible time. So, for me that would probably be number 3, referrals, and 7 and 11. That should do it for me for now. I can always come back to the others later."

"Okay, I know you need to get to your next client so we need to bring this to an end. Are you comfortable with those three for now? Committed to them?"

"Absolutely."

"What I would like to suggest, if you are happy, is that you look at the three with new eyes between now and next time, that you try to go beyond the normal more of the same things we normally put down for these items, but build on them so that the thought of them inspires you. For example, if we look at the term 'referrals' we know what it usually means and is quite bland. But if we build on the concept so that referrals actually become exciting and sexy, well then we might really be onto something. So what kind of referrals would bring this about, for example? What might the best or most exciting referrals be? Which might give you immediate low-hanging fruit? Who can give you referrals that might lead to clients who provide you with solid, consistent orders over a long period? And so on. And once you have these and are satisfied that they are exciting and sexy, well then it's time to build little action plans around those. Perhaps then we can get together in a couple of days to discuss these so that you can take them forward. We shouldn't need more than about fifteen or twenty minutes. Would that be helpful to you?"

"Once again, absolutely," she smiled.

"When do you think you will be in a position to discuss your action plans and list?"

"How are you placed tomorrow afternoon at, say, three?"

"That's good for me. See you then. And good luck with Dr Smith."

5. Shifting the Monkey

"Good morning, Paulo." It was that time of the week again.
"Hi, Tony. How's our sales rep turned manager today?"
"Actually, I am starting to feel that I have begun to make the mind shift – I don't seem to be thinking like a rep any more. It's actually funny: sometimes I stop to check what I am thinking about and it's always manager stuff."
"That's a big shift, even for you," he laughed. "How would you define 'manager stuff'?"
"Well, I seem to catch myself thinking about how I can help a team member do better – how I can 'coax' them, if you like, to shoot the lights out. I never thought I would get so much pleasure out of helping them; I never thought I could do life without selling! In fact, I never thought there was a life beyond selling!"
"'Manager stuff', huh. Tell me more about how you have done this manager stuff with your team – how did you use what you took out of our last discussion to help your team members?"
I spent the next fifteen minutes telling him about the sessions I had had with Liz, Susan and Craig. He listened intently to what I had to say, often checking his understanding and making me think deeper about how I had gone about the 'manager stuff', without ever seeming to judge what I was doing. It was as if his sole purpose was to make me think even more about everything, so much so that at one stage I commented on it.
"Interesting that you should pick up on that. Isn't it all about thinking?" he seemed to ponder, "isn't the ultimate test of what we do about the quality of our thinking and how we develop the quality of thinking in our people?"
"Gee, you have an incredible way of nailing things right on the head," was my automatic response; and then I mirrored his words with a little more thought, "What would be the point of having these conversations with our people if the conversations didn't illicit thought? If we came out of the conversations exactly the same as when we went in? In fact, what is the point of asking questions in these conversations if the questions don't make us think?"

"You see, you're even starting to answer questions with questions – this manager stuff is really sticking, isn't it? So, what kind of manager stuff would you like to discuss today?"

"Actually, I have a pretty difficult conversation I need to have with Linda..."

"Oh, yeah, I've been expecting this to come up sooner or later. What's the purpose, for you, of this particular conversation with her?"

"Well, as you know, her numbers are down. I've only had access to her numbers for the last couple of months but it seems she last hit her target five months ago. Her figures for the last financial year were 70 percent of her target and her year-to-date figures for the first two months of this year are not much better at 75%. I just get the feeling that if I don't do something, she will be happy to operate at this level indefinitely. And it's strange, because on the surface she seems to have so much potential and promise – but she obviously doesn't seem to turn that into results."

"What do you think the main question about her is that you have to answer is?"

"I think it's, do I invest my time in turning her around or am I better off letting her go?"

"That sounds about right. Is she aware of the sensitive nature of her situation? Have you clarified your expectations with her?"

"Well, she is aware of the fact that she's underperforming. I mean she must be. She seems to want to perform."

"Yes, but have you specifically clarified your expectations with her?"

"Well not in so many words. But it's obvious, isn't it?"

"It should be obvious but can you think of anything, just from the stuff you have told me, that might suggest that she might not be exactly on the same page as you?"

"You mean the fact that she seems to have been allowed to underperform for a while?"

"Yes, that might be a good example. What might the impact of that be on your burning question as to whether to invest in her or let her go?"

"Well, I guess it would be a big surprise to her if I start talking about letting her go while all the time she thinks management is okay with her performance track record," I said as I made a note on my, by now, ever-present notebook:

Don't assume. Clarify all expectations

As I wrote it, it flashed across my mind that in most cases it might be necessary to clarify my expectations as well as those of the person I am dealing with.

"Do you want to discuss your burning question?" When I nodded, he continued: "Expand on your conversations with her for me, please."

"Well, we went through the relevant activities which form part of the throughput part of the process you and I discussed last time and looked at the variables, what changes she could make to these, things she could try."

"Have you set her any specific weekly targets around these?'

"No, save that we agreed that her monthly targets are still relevant – and, as I say, different ways she might achieve them."

"How often are you meeting with her?"

"About every ten days to two weeks – I am trying not to give her the idea that I am micromanaging her."

"Let's see. How do you typically hold your team members accountable for their activities?"

"I haven't really thought of it in those terms, I guess. I think I believe that if we agree on something then that is what will or should happen. Sounds terribly naive when I put it that way – is it? When I look at her activity reports, it seems she is there or there about most of the time except there is a lack of consistency. I have explained to her how important it is for her to be organised so that she can be more consistent."

"Do you think this will do it for her?"

"I dunno. I just don't know. I really hope so but I am not sure it will be enough?"

"And if it isn't, what will your next session focus on?"

"Well, it seems a bit pointless to go through her numbers again. I mean, just how many times can I do that? I am sure my predecessors did too. My view – and I am not sure whether you will agree with it – is that we need to have one discussion about it and if her behaviour or underperformance persists, then it needs to be taken to a new level."

"I agree, but why do you think that it should?"

"Wow, let me see. I think maybe it is no longer about the initial behaviour but about the...uh...the pattern. I think it's because a pattern is emerging...and that pattern will stick until something different happens. So something different must happen quickly...and if it doesn't change quickly, then the longer it goes, the less likely it will change. And this doesn't only affect her numbers; it affects the team's and therefore mine. Does that make sense?"

"Absolutely. I would like to come back to the 'something different' in a moment. Before that, can we just spend a moment on your observation that it's not about her initial behaviour anymore but on the pattern. As a rule of thumb, how many times do you think something needs to happen before it becomes a pattern?"

"Gee, we talk so easily about concepts like 'patterns' without ever thinking what it actually means. My immediate answer was going to be three or four times but then I wondered why it isn't that it becomes a pattern on the second time a person does something. Yes, I think that's right."

"And so once it happens a second time, what does your conversation become about: the initial behaviour or the pattern?"

"Thanks, that makes it nice and clear, it becomes about the pattern," I said, making another note:

It is a pattern if it happens twice

Then the conversation becomes about the pattern, not the individual behaviour

"Okay, let's get back to what you said a little earlier: you said 'something different must happen quickly'. So, what would that 'something different' be?"

"I guess I need her commitment firstly. It is not good enough that she just complies with my requests because, unless she is really committed, her performance will just continue to be inconsistent. She must really want to do this, and must commit herself to it.

"Okay, so her commitment to the task at hand is the foundation of your approach. What then?"

"I guess she needs a plan, one that is mapped out step-by-step and has a deadline because we can't just let it go on like it has. I have to get to the stage where I can make a call on whether she will be a consistent performer in the team, even if she is not quite there yet, or whether we need to talk about her other options."

"Good. And how long do you think it would take you to know which decision to make?"

"I reckon I would know in three months, but that's too long – I need to make a call long before then."

"When do you think you need to make a call by?"

"I reckon...one month. Whew, sounds tough. Can we get there in one month?"

"Well, does she have to be performing in one month or do you need to be satisfied that she has turned around sufficiently, firstly, to begin to hit the numbers in a reasonable period and, secondly, once she's there, to do so consistently?

"I guess I need to be satisfied that the trend has changed..oh, the pattern has changed and that she will consistently make the numbers within a short enough period of time."

"Okay, so what would it take for you to get there in a month?"

"Firstly, more frequent meetings. Weekly, no exceptions, no missed meetings on either side."

"Why is that so important to you?"

"Because if we miss meetings, then it may be a message to her that the meetings, and the process, is not as important as she initially was led to believe."

"Good thinking. The most powerful leverage you have under your control is your own behaviour. Everything we do or don't do is a potential message to our people – best we ensure that they get the messages we want them to get." Whew, the wisdom was rolling in this session and I was writing again:

Everything we do or don't do is a potential message to our people

Ensure they get the right message!

"Okay," Paulo continued, "When you are working out the step-by-step plan, how could you ensure that she remains deeply committed?"
"I would let her come up with as much of the strategy as possible, and then when we had put it together, get her commitment to that as well."
"Great. So, through her expressing her commitment, you will have ensured that she is taking responsibility for changing and for sticking to the plan. But let's get back to making her accountable. How could you ensure she's accountable?"
"Okay, it's falling into place now – at least I think so. I think she would be accountable if we discussed what the consequences would be for her if we succeed and if we don't...which brings us back, and answers my initial dilemma: she and I will know whether she should stay or whether we should look at her other options."
"Okay, sounds like you have a plan that will achieve what you want it to achieve. One last thing: we have talked about the steps necessary to hopefully achieve a turnaround or at least know that one is probably on the cards. You also expressed some views earlier about the fact that it has taken so long for Linda to be dealt with. What have you learnt today that might assist you in ensuring that the need for turnaround strategies with reps is less likely to happen in future?"
"As we were talking, I had started thinking about that. It seems to me that this turnaround strategy is just a more intense version of what I should be doing with my team members anyway."

"Sounds like a really good time for you to sum up," he said smiling.

I was already almost at the white board but stopped before I got there. "You know, I think we have left something out. I don't think I will get her real commitment unless she knows that I am committed to help her reach her objectives, if she wants to. So, I am going to add that in."

Turnaround strategy

- Confront with pattern
- Commit to assist, if they are fully committed
- Help them to develop a 4-week step-by-step turnaround plan
  - Use sales process variables
- Obtain commitment to implement plan
- Create accountability
  - Agree consequences of achieving plan objectives and not achieving objectives

3

....

"Hi, Linda. How are you?"

"Fine thanks, Tony. You wanted to see me." I detected a hint of apprehension in her voice. *Not a bad thing,* I found myself thinking. *Nothing like a little creative tension.*

"Yes, Linda. Thanks for responding so promptly. I want to talk to you about our discussion last week. Take a seat." I had consciously decided this would be my home game, for a while anyway, and had moved two chairs from the round table to a position opposite me at my desk.

"You said we would meet again next week," she spurted out defensively. "So, I haven't done all that I said I would do yet – I was going to start tomorrow. I just haven't had the time." It was just rolling out now, making me really pleased Paulo and I had had our discussion.

---

[3] Keith Rosen: Coaching Salespeople into Sales Champions 2008: 270-278

"Don't worry, I know I said we would meet next week. I am sorry, though, that you haven't started your actions yet." She had given me the opportunity and I decided to use it. "I am not sure you understand the urgency of our discussion last week. What do you think will happen if you don't start hitting your numbers, and hitting them consistently, pretty soon?"

"I don't know. No one has ever really said what might happen."

"Still what do *you* think *should* happen?"

"I would really like some more sales skills training - I am sure I would improve if I had some more training."

"Training is an option. But given the period over which you have underperformed now – what's it, at least about five months? – what would *you* do if you were me? How would you deal with you?

"That's hard. I am not you." She said laughing nervously.

"I know. But think about what you would do with you if you were me? In other words, what are the reasonable options open to me?"

"It has been a long time, I know. But I am sure if I just had some more training..."

"I tell you what, Linda," I'd had a brainwave and before I knew it I was standing up and going around the desk, "swap with me. Sit in my chair and I will sit in yours...That's it. Now I want you to think as if you were the manager of the team and I am you – and I have consistently underperformed for more than five months. What is going around in your head as manager?"

She giggled, again nervously, as she realised that I wasn't going to relent on this one. "I guess you want me to say that I would fire you."

"Actually, I don't want you say anything that you wouldn't say if you were the manager in this situation."

A long silence ensued. After what seemed like ages, but was probably about five seconds, I felt tempted to say something just to fill the vacuum. Fortunately, I managed to bite my tongue and focused at looking at her expectantly but without any real emotion.

It worked. "I think...if I was your manager...I would tell me that there isn't a job for you if you don't start hitting your numbers."

"Thank you, Linda. Yes, that is one of my options – and we will get back to that in a moment. What happened to your thinking when you had to act like a manager?"

"I realised that I am responsible for hitting the numbers, no matter what excuses I drum up."

"That's right, Linda. My father always used a metaphor in circumstance like this – about responsibility. You've probably heard it: what has happened is that you, and I, have allowed your monkey to jump from your shoulder onto mine. When that happens I need to ask: Whose monkey is it? If it is mine, then I need to take responsibility for it. If it is yours, then I need to make sure you keep the monkey. As I see it, it is your responsibility – or monkey – to hit the numbers. My monkey is to help you achieve that without taking back the responsibility for hitting the numbers. Does that make sense?"

"Yeah. It seems so obvious when you put it that way."

"Okay, what is my responsibility as far as the team and as far as my superiors are concerned?"

"Um...to make sure everyone hits their numbers?"

"That's right, because the team and the organisation are affected by it, not so? It also means I will not hit my numbers if team members don't hit theirs. So, what is my responsibility to them and to myself when someone consistently doesn't hit those numbers?"

"It seems like you would need to help until you think you were wasting your time and then you would need to make a decision in the best interests of the team and the organisation."

"You are really starting to think like a manager now so, before you get too comfortable in my chair, let's go and sit at the round table." When we sat down, I continued. "Okay, you were right, Linda. I am at the stage where we either need to turn your performance around in a very short time, or we will need to talk about your options. Would that be fair to you, and to the whole team?"

She nodded, looking down to avoid eye contact.

"Okay," I continued. "I would like to say firstly that it is up to you. I would like nothing more than to help you not only turn your performance around, but for you to consistently be one of our top reps. And if that's what you want to do, I will do everything in my power to help get you there. But I know that selling is a tough job – rewarding, yes, but tough – and if you feel you are not up to it, then I won't think any less of you if you say so, and we can look at what your best options are. How do you feel about what I am saying?"

"I have been so scared that I would be fired that I haven't been able to do anything – I haven't been able to think about anything else but what I would do if you did fire me. I have been so confused."

"Okay, so how do you feel about what I have said then?"

"I think I am relieved. I mean I know there is still a lot of work in front of me if I am going to salvage my job, but your offering to help me get there means a lot. So, if you are asking me if I want to give it a go, then yes, I would...and thank you for taking this approach."

"If you are willing and able to give it a go, then I will support you 100 percent. The question is then, just how much do you want this?"

"Tony, I would like for nothing more than to get out of this inertia, this feeling of failure – it's just not me; I have never failed at anything before. So, I want this badly."

"Yes, but how badly?"

"Tony, I know I can do this job and can do it well. I want to show you, I want to show the team, that I can do this job. Mostly, I want to show myself."

"The fact that you have been so scared that you haven't been able to do anything suggests to me that your confidence is down. Whilst your heart is in the right place, I am also not sure that your efforts and activities have been aimed in the right direction. As I have said, and I want you to know this, I am fully committed to supporting you and helping you to start meeting your numbers. But, what's more important is your commitment to wanting to do this. And you have given me that commitment, haven't you?"

"Yes, I really want this; and I will do whatever is necessary, I assure you."

"Okay, so this is what we are going to do. Together we will set the outcomes that we want you to achieve over the next four weeks. We'll also develop a step-by-step plan that we agree will turn around your performance within the next four weeks if you stick to your commitment and achieve each of the milestones. We will meet weekly to discuss your progress against the action plan and, at the end of the four week period, we will meet and together decide what the best course of action for you will be. That could be building on your success over this period or talking about your options outside of your present role, either with this organisation or another. Is this process something you are willing to commit to? Remember, if you would rather be out now, I will think no less of you and will help you think about your future. So, if that is an attractive option for you, now would be a good time to raise it. But if you are committed as you say you are, then I will commit to helping you. So, what do you want to commit to?" It felt like I was really belabouring this but I wanted to be really sure, firstly, of her commitment levels and, secondly, that there was no room for misunderstanding.

Linda was thoughtful for a little while. "No, Tony, I am in. I really want this. And I am grateful for the opportunity you have given me."

"Okay, then, let's get started. I have got another hour before my next meeting. Are you happy that we spend that time putting the step-by-step action plan together?"

Linda nodded, and we got underway. I asked her to explain to me in detail how she went about her role as a rep, what she did on a daily basis. As she explained this to me I glanced at my notes I had written down to help me probe deeply enough for us to get a thorough understanding of what was going on:

S.C.R.O.I.P. - probing for

- *specifics*
- *clarification*
- her *rationale* for doing or saying something
- *options*
- the *impact* or consequences of her thinking or actions
- her *perspectives* or beliefs about what she was saying and the possible perspectives or beliefs of the other people involved

4

---

[4] Adapted from Dorothy Strachan: Making Questions Work 2007: 59-65

I have always had the sense that, given half a chance, we tend to express ourselves superficially – stay on the surface - and that I needed to, as much as possible, and without interrogating her, move her deeper in her thinking, from the general to the more *specific*. I tried to focus on her specific actions whenever she dealt with anything superficially or through generalisation, I tried to prompt her to be more specific, to go deeper and wider in terms of her thinking. I asked her for specific examples and found that she would still come up with general trends or intentions but I kept at it until I got the specific detailed examples I asked for. From time to time, I asked her to *clarify* what she was saying so that I could be sure I had got it right. On other occasions I asked her for her *rationale* in doing things so that we could both be clear on her reasons and she might have an opportunity to reconsider them. When it seemed to me that she might not have considered the various *options* open to her before she decided on a course of action, I asked her if she was faced with the same circumstances again, what other options she might consider, no matter how stupid these might sound, and kept her at it until we had at least five or six options so that she could get in the habit of scanning for options and thereby making better decisions. Sometimes, when I thought she hadn't thought things through sufficiently I asked her to provide me with the *impact* or consequences of what she was saying on the client, herself, the team, or the organisation. Finally, I tried to understand what she was saying, and tried to help her to look at what she was relating, from the *perspectives* of the various players involved.

"Okay," I said when we were finished. "Thank you for sharing all that with me; it really helps me to understand. I hope it helped you to crystallise your thoughts too?" She nodded wide-eyed. I then summarised what she and I had concluded were the main issues. She confirmed that my summary was accurate.

'Linda, which of these issues do you think needs to be dealt with first? Which is the most important?"

"Do you mean important in terms of urgent?"

"No, I mean in terms of which issue, if we resolved it properly, would take you closer to your goal of making your numbers?"

"Well, at this stage I don't think it is going to help in the short run – in our four weeks – if I qualify new prospects because the process of converting them into sales is too long. So I think it is a toss-up between making more calls and getting sales in those calls. Can't I do both?"

"In this instance, I think you can because they complement each other." We then continued to look at as many different ways that she could think of to get the number of her calls up. I tried to stretch her to think outside of the hardy annuals she had always used or that sales people normally come up with. When she rejected some of her own suggestions, I suggested that we not judge the options she was generating and that we merely generate as many as possible without entering into a discussion about any of them. In the end we had nine options on the table. I asked her which of the options that would make the biggest difference she could implement immediately, given the fact that she had four weeks to turn her performance around.

"Good," I summarised. "So, we have two things that you are going to put in place. You said immediately but when exactly will you start them?" She replied that she would start the two actions immediately after the meeting. "Linda, what happens when we meet as agreed next week and you haven't done what you said you would?"

"I know, I haven't exactly built up a good track record around walking the talk, have I?"

"Regardless of the past, Linda, I just want to know how we will deal with anything like that during this four week process. So what would happen?" I had noticed that she had a wonderful ability to deflect direct questions, wittingly or unwittingly. She enjoyed vague spaces but I was determined to get accountability.

At that moment she seemed to realise that she was at the crossroads – she had no option but to go worst-case scenario because we were in zero tolerance mode. "I guess that if that happens my commitment today will have meant nothing. So you should withdraw your investment in me and, I suppose, we would be discussing my future in a different role, inside or outside the company."

"Are you okay with that?"

She paused. "I don't really have much option - I have committed myself and so, yes, I am okay with that."
Accountability at last!
"Good," I said, standing up. "I will hear from you this afternoon then." My first really tough conversation as a sales manager was over. *You know what,* I heard myself saying to myself,

> Tough conversations are not that tough if you set them up properly.

6. Joint Learning

Susan and I met in the car park on the dot of 12pm the next day as arranged. She had arranged for us to see two customers that afternoon.

I had thought I would prepare her along the way for an approach I was exploring for joint calls, an approach that seemed to make sense to me but differed from that of my predecessors. "Susan, we've both been on joint calls with sales managers before but I would like to try something a little different this afternoon."

"What do you mean?" she responded somewhat nervously.

"Don't worry," I said. "I don't want to change anything from the client's perspective so I will come along as an observer."

"An observer. What do you mean?" she repeated.

"Relax. I know that we have both had sales managers in the past that took over on these joint visits. I would rather not do that. Can we explore a few reasons why, from the client's perspective, this approach might be more ideal?"

She nodded. "I suppose it's confusing for the client. In fact, I have always felt it is. The client deals with me and has the relationship with me and then someone else comes in and takes over for one meeting and then goes off into the sunset, leaving the client feeling like they are part of an experiment – or part of a Punch and Judy show."

"I can see you feel strongly about this. It is confusing to the client – *and* it undermines your relationship with them. What are we trying to achieve in a normal joint visit?"

"I have always thought it was to help the sales rep become more effective?"

"Yes, I think that's exactly right. Which would help you more - you observing me conducting the meeting or by me observing you?"

"Well, I thought it would be by me observing you, but I have a feeling that's not the answer you're looking for." She was starting to relax a little, starting to be herself, letting her sense of humour sneak through.

"You're right. You and I have different personalities so, whilst there is a sales process, our different personalities take us through the sales process differently, in ways that fit those personalities more comfortably. If we didn't do it like this, we would come across with a lack of authenticity, and we would lose more sales than we should. Also, I hardly know the clients we are seeing this afternoon – we have no relationship or understanding – and this fact, together with the fact that the meeting is a one-off, puts a completely unnatural dynamic into the mix."

"But you've been so successful. I am sure I could learn a lot from you."

"Even if it meant doing things in a way that feels strange to you?"

"I guess you're right."

We had arrived at our destination. "Why don't you do the first one in the same way you would normally do it? I will observe and I will give you feedback over a cup of coffee afterwards – I see we have some time in between meetings. If it works for you, then we carry on the same way. If not, we'll discuss how we can do it so it works better for you. How does that sound?"

I think she knew by now that I was unlikely to budge on this one. "Okay, let me just get my thoughts together for a moment."

So far so good.

....

"Okay, that was pretty painless," I smiled as we sat down in the coffee shop after the meeting with client.

"For you, maybe," she quipped, "but I was the one in the hot seat."

We ordered two cappuccinos. "Tell me what worked for you."

She thought for a moment – which I was starting to realise was the point of these conversations. "Well, I think I have a good relationship with him. I always think that is a good start."

"I agree," I said. "Still, what evidence do you have of the fact that you have a good relationship? What are the things you noticed in this regard?"

"Gee, I don't know...When I introduced you, he cracked a lame joke about it being time someone kept an eye on me...And he teased me once or twice after that."

"That's right. He also used supportive language to suggest that he rates you. What else worked for you?"

"Yes, I suppose you are right now that you mention it. Well, he bought some product...that's definitely a plus. Apart from that, I don't really know, except that it seemed a really relaxed meeting."

"Yes, it was relaxed, and that is probably one of your strengths, getting people to relax in your company. Okay, what didn't work for you?"

"At one stage, I felt we might have been talking past each other."

"Would you like to give me an example of what you mean?"

"I don't know, it felt as if my responses to some of the stuff he said missed the point he was trying to make."

"Can you give me a specific example?" I pressed.

"He was talking about the operation he conducted this morning and when I started to talk about our gauzes, there seemed to be an uncomfortable silence."

"Yes, would you like to hazard a guess as to what happened there?"

"Umm...when I think about it, my feeling uncomfortable only disappeared when we talked about sutures. I don't know what happened there."

"Take me through your thoughts during that period of the conversation."

"Well, he was talking away – he does go on a bit, doesn't he – about the patient bleeding after he had sown her up so I thought we could solve that with a better quality gauze."

"Could you have made an assumption here?"

"What do you mean?"

"Could you have assumed that he was talking about gauze when in actual fact he might have been talking about the quality of the sutures?"

"Gee, I hadn't thought of that. That's probably right, because he brought the conversation back to sutures a few times , and I think I persisted with gauze for a while and it was only when I started to ask him what he meant about sutures that we seemed to get back onto the same page."

"You mentioned that you felt some discomfort during this part of the visit. Did this discomfort continue after you got on the same page?"

"No, now that you mention it, I remember feeling a sense of relief."

"So, what do you learn from this?"

"To check my assumptions."

"And how might you have done that in this instance?"

"I suppose I could've checked with him what he thought the cause of the bleeding was or what he had in mind."

"Yes, that would have worked. Can you think of any other assumptions you may have made during the meeting?"

"Now that I think of it, I assumed that because he had run out of XP203 that he was going to place an order for that but then he ordered half the amount but of the cheaper XP199. That wasn't so great. Oh yes, then there was also..." and she proceeded to list another three assumptions. "Seems like I make a lot of assumptions," she concluded.

"At least you are becoming aware of it and that it might be a habit. What is the impact of this habit for you?"

"Well, this morning it cost me nearly R50 000 with the XP199's alone – and perhaps there were other examples of missed sales or down-selling."

"So, how can you ensure that you make a practice of checking your assumptions?"

A long silence ensued. Eventually, she asked: "Have I made any assumptions in our conversation now?"

"I don't really know. What are you getting at?"

"Well, maybe I make assumptions in all my conversations – I probably don't reserve them just for sales conversations. If that's the case, then...oh dear, I think that was another assumption! At least it answers the question. I do make assumptions in different conversations and what I can do is exactly what I did just now."

I had a feeling that she was about to lose me so I tentatively put a "What do you mean?" on the table.

"Don't you see?" she said. "When I asked you whether I had made any assumptions in our conversation now, I was checking my assumption that I might have made assumptions in our conversation. So, that's what I must do: get into the habit of checking as many of my assumptions as possible. Do you think that will work? Get it," she laughed, "I think I just checked another."

"It might work, yes. Why don't you try it for a week and then we will see just how effective it has been?" She nodded enthusiastically. "What about the change to XP199's?" I asked. "How did you respond?"

"Not well, I am afraid. I was so dumbfounded that I just let it go."

"If we look back at that moment, with the benefit of hindsight, what other possible responses might you have tried? Perhaps you could brainstorm some options."

"I suppose I could've asked him what the hell he wanted to do that for," she giggled. She seemed to be enjoying herself quite a lot for someone who had just left some money – and commission – on the table.

"Yes, that's one option. What else?"

With prompting, she came up with several possibilities and we then decided on an approach that enquired into what problem the client thought would be better served by this product and their thinking behind that choice.

When we had finished brainstorming, she continued:

"There was something else I think I learnt but I am not sure what it was. Do we have time to flesh it out a little?"

"Sure, do you think we can deal with it effectively in three or four minutes?"

"I think so. It has to do with some of the feelings I had. You asked me if my feelings of discomfort stopped at about the time that he and I were on the same page again and I said it did, and that I remembered feeling relief. Could that mean anything? Is there something I could learn from this?"

"What do you think you might be able to learn from this?"

"To listen to my body. Surely if I am feeling uncomfortable then something is wrong – as it was in this case. Also, my sense of relief signalled to me that things were okay. As I speak, it seems to me that the feelings I have might provide me with clues as to what is going on."

"Perhaps it would help you to elaborate on this line of thinking."

"Well, my discomfort was a warning that things were not okay, and my sense of relief told me that things were back on track."

"That's pretty perceptive of you. So, what do you want to take away from this?"

"That maybe I should trust my feelings, my intuition. Maybe I need to check in with what I am feeling from time to time and use my feelings to inform how I proceed. Gee, I think that's powerful."

"I think it is too. I don't think you will find it in many sales skills textbooks but I think you have hit on something that could be really useful to you. What do you need to do with this now?"

"I would like to consciously check my feelings two or three times a sales call, even jot them down quickly, and then afterwards consider what was happening in the conversation at the time of those feelings. Then, perhaps we can keep this as an item on the agenda to discuss next time."

"Sure. That sounds great. To a large extent the agenda for these discussions belongs to you, so please feel free to raise anything you believe will help you become more effective. Okay," I said, looking at my watch. "Time to hit the road."

"There's something else that worked for me," she said with a hint of a smile on her face as we climbed into the car.

"What's that?"

"Well, two simple, basic questions led to quite a lot of discussion back there."

"What were they?"

"What worked for you?"

"What didn't?"

....

The next meeting seemed to pass more quickly than the first, even though we were with the client for the same amount of time. On my way to the car, I glanced at the new framework I was going to try in our conversation on the way home. It was really simple so I wondered for a moment why I needed the reassurance of the glance. Simply, it read:

What did you notice?

What did you notice?

Of the things you noticed, what stands out for you?

Tell me more...

Susan tried to pre-empt me, and it nearly succeeded in distracting me from the process. "Gee, Tony, I am sorry, that didn't go well. I just seemed so nervous."

"Do you think it generally didn't go well, or is there something specific you are referring to?"

"I wasn't happy about the whole meeting, but think it got worse when she seemed to resist all my efforts to get a sale. As I say, the whole meeting didn't flow well – for some reason, I seemed to be really nervous. Then later I didn't respond well to the resistance."

Remembering my chats with Paulo around interference and the sales process model, I asked: "Which would you like to talk about first: your nerves or the resistance?"

"I think the resistance. That's where I really blew the sale."

"Okay," I said, relieved that I could now get back on track. "What are the various things you noticed about her resistance?"

"She seemed to have made up her mind before we started."

"At this stage, I think it would benefit us more to focus on the actual things you noticed – rather than any interpretations you may place on those things - that led you to your conclusion that she had made up her mind before we started."

"Gee, that's really hard. It is just what I felt."

"I know, but play the video back in your mind of what you noticed her saying or doing during that stage of the meeting. What are the various things you noticed?"

"She's normally pretty friendly but she was quite short and formal with us right from the start."

"Good. What else did you notice?"

"That's what threw me, her changed behaviour got my nerves going and I never quite recovered."

"Okay, what else did you notice?"

"She wasn't really prepared to consider what I was saying."

"Is that what you noticed or did something you notice lead to that conclusion?"

"I suppose it's a conclusion. What led me to that?" I was pleased to see her asking herself questions. Somehow, I (deeply) felt that the more she (and the other reps) asked themselves questions, the better their performance would be.

"Oh, every time I tried to sell her the benefits of our product, she compared it to an opposition product. I remember wondering whether the reps from the other companies had somehow beaten me to the draw."

"Was there anything specific you noticed about the products she was referring to or the argument she was making about them?"

"Not really, I think I started to panic – I kept just trying to find more benefits from our product that would trump the benefits of the opposition products."

"So, are you saying you noticed that you panicked?"

"Yes, I guess so. I guess that's right."

"Anything else?"

"Well, now that I think back and see it unfolding in the video, I stopped listening to her."

"Okay, so you've noticed that she wasn't as friendly as usual, this made you nervous, she kept countering the benefits you were giving her with stuff about the opposition products, you panicked, and the more you panicked the less you listened to her. Would that be an accurate summary?"

"Spot on, I'm afraid."

"Is there anything else you noticed that we should add?"

"No, I think that's it."

"Okay, of the things you have noticed, which one stands out for you?"

"Gee, they are all important. I guess the fact that I became so nervous."

"That makes sense. You seem to go back to that one quite often. Tell me more – what makes it stand out for you?"

"Firstly, the fact that I was thrown so easily by her formality and brevity. I just seemed to stutter along after that. Things went from bad to desperate until in the end I simply wasn't listening to her."

"It is interesting for me that, whilst you see her formality and brevity as a catalyst, you don't seem to be blaming her. You are almost blaming yourself. Am I reading you right?"

"Yes, I think so. I hadn't noticed that. Was it her fault or mine?"

"Do you think one of you needs to be at fault?"

By this time, we had got back to the office and were seating ourselves at the round table in my office.

"No, I can't put my finger on it but it doesn't seem as if fault is relevant here – even if I was becoming fairly angry by the end. Mind you, she could probably sense that I wasn't listening to what she had to say – she probably felt unheard."

The level of the conversation energised me. Quite unexpectedly, we seemed to be operating at a really deep level with insights almost pouring out for both of us. I tried to contain my excitement but the positive energy in the room was tangible for both of us.

"She may well have felt that – and I am glad that you have, in this moment, taken the time to see it from her point of view as well. If fault isn't relevant here, what might be? What do we need to be mindful of regarding the dynamic between the two of you during the meeting, if it is not fault?" I realised that for the umpteenth time in this session, I didn't know the answer to my own question. The strange thing was that, whereas this would normally make me feel vulnerable – being the know-all that I am – it was this very fact that was creating the excitement within me: I was learning stuff at so many levels it was almost scary.

"I guess it is that we each played a role in what happened. So, she was formal and brief, I got nervous, she got defensive (if that's the right word), I panicked and stopped listening."

"Sorry, I am a little visual;" I said getting up and walking to my ever-helpful white board."But maybe it will help us both if I draw this – I am not quite sure what yet! – on the board. What I am hearing you say, firstly, is that this is not a linear thing about blame – you were not pointing fingers at each other like this:

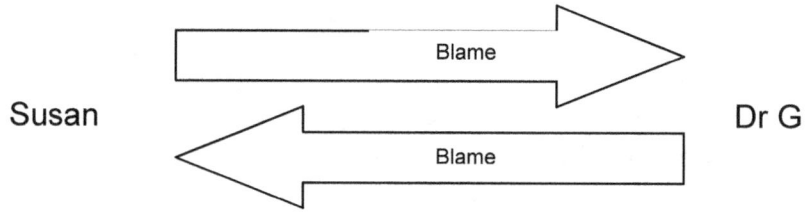

Does that make sense to you?"

"Yes, it does."

"Then, the fault thing," I was still making this up as I went, "seems to be more round and round, cyclical, more systemic – perhaps like this:

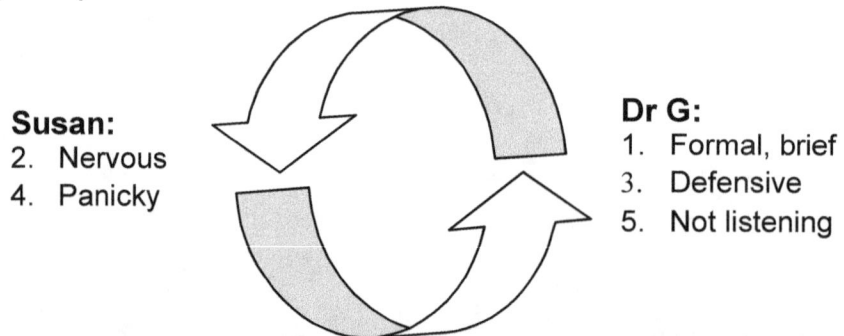

Are we still on the same page – well, white board?"
"Absolutely," and with that I knew for certain that she felt energised too. "Except that maybe it didn't start with #1. Maybe something happened before that made her respond by being formal and brief."
"Okay, let's explore that. Would that have been something you did – sorry, played a role in?"
"Not necessarily, although it may have been something like her feeling ambushed with my boss and I outnumbering her, or it could have been something I did last time. But it could have been something that happened to her earlier today or whenever – maybe she is just having a bad hair day."
"But it made you feel...?"
"Nervous."
"Why do you think it made you feel nervous?" I had a feeling we were easing into the "interference" item on our agenda.
"I know exactly why. I immediately felt responsible. I thought I had done something that had put her in a bad mood. Oops!"
"What?"
"Well, I made an assumption, didn't I? And I didn't check my assumption."
"You're getting good at this. Something tells me that the more you become aware of occasions when you act out this pattern, the better you will get at preventing it. In this case, however, what do you think caused you to make this assumption?"
"Oh, I know the answer to that. I have done it all my life. I take things personally."
"And how does that work for you, taking things personally?"
"Never well. In this case, it caused me to get nervous, to panic, not listen and probably lose a sale."
"So, what do you think the solution is for you?"
"It seems that two things have rung very loud and clear today". Surprisingly, she went up to the white board and wrote on it, almost as if to publish the fact to the world, but also to warn that world:

Don't take things personally

Don't make assumptions

"That makes sense, Susan. And they are lessons we should all remember. So, how will you remember to do these things?" "Yeah, they look so simple on the board, but to consistently implement them is more difficult. I think I will buy myself a small notebook, or even a journal, and try to record after as many sales meetings with clients as possible each day how I scored on each of those items. In fact, it isn't just sales meetings; I should do this exercise after every conversation I have, or as often as possible. I wonder how I could remember to record this after every conversation?" She was asking herself this question so I remained quiet, confident that she would find the solution. She didn't let me down – in fact, she didn't let herself down! After about five seconds, which seemed like ages, she continued: "I know, for each of the sales meetings I will take the journal out and put it with my other stuff. That will then also serve as a reminder not to take things personally and not to make assumptions during that meeting. I see on average four or five clients a day so it will become more a part of my life and I am more likely to increasingly remember to make notes after other informal conversations. Also, perhaps I could read through the journal every evening, perhaps work through the day in my head and include some of the conversations I might have forgotten. That way, I can check for any patterns that set my assumptions of sensitivity off and see what might help me the next day. I am sure that if I did that for say four weeks – it's nearly the end of this month, so say from now until the end of next month – new patterns that work better for me will have emerged."

It wasn't the way I would have done it. I was about to share my way with her when I realised that her way might work for her and that my mere preferences were probably irrelevant in the circumstances. I corrected myself, correctly as it turned out! "That sounds good. Pretty comprehensive. It seems to me that it's really difficult for us to break bad habits and replace them with more effective habits or practices – but I think you have done a pretty good job there. Let's see if I have it right: You will keep a journal to record after every conversation how you have gone in terms of making assumptions and taking things personally; to ensure you remember and to reinforce the lesson you will place the journal with your other items like pens etc on the desk or table at these meetings; and you will read through what you have written every evening. Do I have it right?" She nodded enthusiastically. "Is there anything I can do to support you in this?"

"Could we put it on the agenda for our weekly meetings for at least the next four or five weeks and then we can decide what we need to do with the item at that stage?"

"Of course, would it help you if we made you responsible for raising the item at our meetings?"

"That's a good idea. Yes. Adds a little tension to the process!" she smiled.

"Okay, we have spoken about a lot of really 'soft skill' stuff today. What effect do you think the stuff you have learnt today will have on your numbers?"

"Well, for starters, in both meetings I left a hell of a lot of money on the table. If I am making a habit of that, even smaller amounts, then my numbers should go up if my strategy in the sales conversations with clients is more...more...well, accurate and...effective. I think there will also be a spin-off in areas where I might generally be pretty good at the moment, so my numbers – which are generally okay – are likely to go up even more."

"Sounds good to me." I had no doubt she was right.

"To me too!"

"That's about it for today from my side. We don't have time to go through our normal wrap up, the stuff that stood out for you today and to summarise your actions, so would you mind putting them in an email for me so that we stay on the same page."

"Sure, I will do it before I leave. Thanks a lot, Tony. I have had an awesome day." And with that she bounced out of my office.

7. Don't fudge the process

9 am. It was time for my session with Paulo. I knocked on his open door and he immediately stood up, welcomed me – *was he really that pleased to see me?* – and beckoned me to his round table.

"Hey, what's up, Tony? You seem to have something on your mind."

"Is it that obvious?" I retorted. At first I had wondered why I felt a little anxious that morning and then, thinking about it, realised that my session later with Linda could potentially see me 'fire' my first employee. "I am a little concerned. Remember, I mentioned the session I had with Linda last week and that she had committed herself to the four week plan you and I had developed? Well, I have seen some activity and there's a slight increase in her sales numbers but I am pretty sure this leopard hasn't changed her spots. And I guess I am nervous in case I have to follow through with option 2."

"What makes you think she hasn't fulfilled her commitments?"

"It's more of a feeling really. She just doesn't seem like the consistent sort. She can be quite flighty. I just don't think she can sustain any effort she might be making."

"Sometimes one's intuition can be helpful. Do you think it is being helpful in this instance?'

"Not really. I seem to be pre-occupied with this."

"What kind of energy do you think you are expending on this – positive or negative?"

"Negative, definitely. It feels draining."

"What do you think is causing that negative energy?"

"Linda's inconsistent track record?" I queried apologetically.

"A track record is in the past, isn't it? By definition. What do you think is causing it right now?"

"I am scared that she is going to repeat the pattern I see." This time I was a little more confident in my reply.

"So, the negative energy is based more on your fear than on anything she is actually doing right now?" he checked.

"I guess so."

"What do you have control over at this moment?"

"My fear, I suppose I could manage it better. In fact, you are right – I can't do anything about what she may or may not have done at this stage."

"What is that fear about, Tony?"

"I am scared that I might have to get rid of her, effectively fire her."

"If we walked you through that possibility today so that you might be better prepared if it does happen, would that be the most effective use of our time together this morning?"

"Absolutely. That would be great."

"Okay. What are you really fearful of?"

"Getting rid of someone seems so...well...final. Isn't there any other way?"

"Well, let's consider whether there is any other way. Do you have any other ways in mind?"

"Not really. By making her commit to her actions and then ensuring she is accountable by getting her to commit to the outcomes if she doesn't follow through, I feel a little locked in – damned if I do, damned if I don't. I mean if she hasn't tried, then I agree, that's it. But what if she has tried really hard but hasn't made anything like the number of calls she committed to, or she is just short, or she is just short and would've made it but for the unavailability of a couple of her clients? What if..."

"Whoa. Let's have a look at this. But first let me say that your empathy and caring for her is to be commended. If you were able to be totally callous about the possible route you might need to go, I would be worried. But let's go back to the facts, brutal as they are. You made a decision to pursue this turnaround route last week – what facts did you base this decision on?"

"A track record of consistent underperformance. Yes, I know..."

"But let's double check anyway. It might make you feel better. Has anything changed regarding her underperformance?"

"Well, she is still underperforming although her numbers are slightly up this week."

"What are your expectations of her performance for this four week programme?"

"We agreed that it was almost impossible for her to get her numbers consistently on target in four weeks and that the best we could expect is a positive trend. If the trend suggests that she is going to hit her numbers consistently in the near future, then she's okay. If not, then we look at options."

"So, for today's purposes, her numbers are not so important?"

"No. What is important," I said trying to anticipate his next question "is that she is held accountable for what she agreed to do, which is to hit the number of calls to clients."

"So, your concern is only if she didn't hit the number of calls?"

"Well, that's what she held herself accountable for."

"What is your expectation behind the number of calls? Are you hoping to see anything else?"

"Yes, effort. Energy. Attitude. I think that's what I really want to see. If those are sufficiently up, the numbers – calls, sales, everything – will go up fairly soon."

"So if she doesn't hit the numbers but shows genuine positive change in effort, energy and attitude, this would please you?"

"Yes, thanks, it's starting to get a little clearer."

Paulo kept quiet for a while so I continued. "I suppose this goes back to the 'what-ifs' I was ranting off earlier. If there is genuine effort etc and the numbers are a little disappointing, especially if clients have come in with some late cancellations or excuses, if she has done all in her power, then that would be acceptable to me. It's not just about the number of calls – her commitment was really about a change in attitude and approach."

"There are some intangibles here. It may be difficult to measure her performance in those areas. Do you think that you will know if she has achieved the standard you are setting, or would you like to develop this further?"

"No, I think I get it now. I still feel a little anxious though."

"What's that about, do you think?"

"It's still a very difficult conversation."

"The stuff we have talked about is probably the 'what'; I think what you are talking about now is the 'how'. Does this sound right?"

"Yes, I guess I need assurance that I can do this, if I have to, with the minimum amount of conflict or hurt."

"Yes, I see that. I often find that we confuse the 'what' and the 'how' – and you may in fact have found yourself doing just that a little earlier – where, because the 'how' is such a difficult conversation (or we think it will be), we start rationalising on why we should avoid the 'what'. What, excuse the pun," (always the joker, Paulo was, but I found the focused informality of these sessions so energising), 'we have done here is to separate the two parts of the conversation – if the 'what' is correct in principle, which I think is the point that we have arrived at here, then we have to find a way to confront the challenge of doing the difficult 'how' with the minimum amount of conflict and hurt, as you said. If the 'what' is right, we need to find the right way to do the 'how'. But whilst we continue to confuse the 'what' and the 'how', it all seems way too difficult."

"That's very useful. Do you mind if I summarise and make notes of where we are at before we go on."

"Not at all. Would you like to read it out to me as you go?" I nodded.

- Focus on what you have control over
- Distinguish between the 'what' and the 'how'
- If the 'what' is right in principle, find a win-win way to achieve the 'how'
- The harder the 'how', the more considerate and caring, but fair I need to be

"That sounds good," Paulo continued. "What do you think the characteristics are of giving difficult feedback. What do you think you need to make sure you do this afternoon if this becomes a difficult conversation?"

"Well, if I were to put myself in her shoes, I would be nervous about telling my manager I didn't do what I committed to do – if we assume my assumption is correct for the moment! So, I would hope that it would be a discussion rather than a battle. By that I mean, and it may just be me, that I would hope that we wouldn't have a shouting match or that the boss would be able to control any anger they may have."

"Okay, but what would then need to happen at the beginning of the conversation?"

"Sorry, before I answer that, that's the point I was trying to make. It's got to still be a conversation, no matter how tough the conversation or topic is."

"Good point, it *is* still just a conversation. Okay, back to my question: what could you do at the beginning to ensure that the conversation gets off to a good start?"

"For me, I think, it is important that I prepare beforehand and that I don't wing it. If I don't prepare, there is every chance that I could say something that makes her defensive. So, it is important that I don't over-react in any way."

"How might your over-reaction manifest itself?"

"It might be in the words I say, in my body language, the expression on my face, things like that. I guess I need to make sure that I act and feel the same as I normally do when I have sessions with my team members. Obviously, if I just attack from the outset, if I come across aggressive in any way, I am going to have a very difficult conversation."

"So, what is the opposite of 'attack' or 'aggressive' for you in these circumstances? If it helps, complete this sentence: 'The setup needs to be...'"

"Uh...'gentle' comes to mind, but at the same time focused or purposeful."

"Okay, so are we talking about a 'gentle yet purposeful setup'?"

"Yes, that's it. It's no good just being gentle and beating around the bush, it's no good avoiding the issue."

"So, in this instance, what would 'a gentle and purposeful setup sound like'? Let's role play it."

"You mean use the actual words? Okay...I think it would go something like this: 'Linda, last week we agreed and you committed to a four week turnaround plan. As the first part of that plan, you committed to doing two things during the past week: seeing four clients every day, that's twenty in the week; and to set up some joint visits. I see we have three joint visits set up for tomorrow, great, so that's taken care of. How did you go on the first commitment?'"

"Good, so how would you rate that out of ten as a gentle yet purposeful setup?"

"Yeah, I am quite happy with that for a first time. Probably an eight or nine. I think it would be effective."

"What is the point of making it 'purposeful' for you?"

"I think it's about ensuring that one doesn't fudge the process. It is so easy to focus on a gentle setup, or even a gentle conversation, and the team member doesn't get the message because we've been too soft and vague and...general. Purposeful makes it focused and more specific – they must get the message."

"What is the message always about: the person or their behaviour?"

"Oh, I get it; therefore it is about the behaviour. Good point, so in the conversation I should be careful not to make personal remarks – I must focus only on the behaviour, not the person."

"Okay, so you have decided to prepare, use a gentle yet purposeful setup, not to fudge your message and to focus on the behaviour not the person. What other guidelines would you give me if I was to be going into one of these conversations?"

"Well, I think it has to do with the fact that so many people seem to feel it has to be an aggressive discussion, with some shouting included just for the hell of it."

"So, what would you suggest I substitute instead of the shouting?" he laughed.

"I just don't think it is necessary to shout to get your point across. It should be enough to be firm but fair. So, it's a focused conversation and you shouldn't allow it to go off course, to get distracted with arguments on some detail. Quietly, but firmly and fairly bring the conversation back on course when that happens. That's what I think, anyway."

"But what about those factual arguments? What happens if you start disagreeing about the facts?"

"I think that's where your preparation comes in again. You should know your facts when you go into the conversation and, if necessary, have the facts to back them up. The last thing you want is to get sidetracked."

"Okay, back to you again. Is there anything else you think you might need from our discussion to prepare you for your conversation with Linda?"

I glanced at my notes:

- Prepare
- Gentle yet purposeful setups
- Don't fudge the message
- Focus on behaviour, not the person
- Be firm but fair
- Know the facts
- Stick to the facts

"No," I said, "I feel a whole lot more comfortable about it. I think I was most scared about getting distracted on some arbitrary point and that would frustrate me and could lead to me getting angry."

"Anger is a difficult challenge sometimes, isn't it? We all get angry and I haven't noticed it being a particular problem for you. But it's what we do to manage it that's important. Would you like to talk about it quickly?"

I looked at my watch. "Will it take longer than eight minutes?"

"Shouldn't. Okay?"

"Sure."

"Okay, let me cut to the quick to speed things up. What happens immediately before you lose your temper?"

"I feel myself getting flushed, and then I lose it."

"You feel yourself getting flushed," he repeated. "Every time?"

"I think so – I can't say that I have consciously checked. But when you asked me I could almost feel the warmness flow through my body like it does when I get flushed."

"Do you think you could, in future, consciously check for that feeling? And if you could, do you think you could use it as a warning, an alarm or red flag?"

"I think I could if I kept my wits about me but the point is that we lose it at the moment we can't keep our wits about us."

"Let's focus on that moment for a moment," he smiled again. He had a wonderful ability to make the most serious of topics fun to discuss. "Think carefully, does anything happen in that moment before you lose it? Do you say anything to yourself?"

"I have never thought about that but, now that you mention it, I know that I say something like 'stuff this' or 'that's enough'."

"Good, what do you think those words signify for you in that moment?"

"It's like...," a bright light went on in my mind as it suddenly became so clear to me. "It's like I have just given myself permission to lose it. That's it, isn't it. We talk in terms of losing it as if it is a natural consequence of what precedes that moment. But I reckon I give myself permission to lose it." I was stunned by this new awareness and sat there reflecting on it. If Paulo was keen to get into the conversation at this point, it certainly didn't seem that way and we sat in silence for probably fifteen seconds. I was learning that silences in the midst of a conversation seem to create vacuums, because vacuums always suck stuff into them – I am sure my science teacher at school put it more eloquently. The current vacuum began to whisper, at first, but by the end of the fifteen seconds the voice was very loud in my head: *And so?...And so?...And so?* So much so, that without thinking, I suddenly heard myself speaking. "And so, if I can give myself permission to lose it, I can also withhold that permission – I can refuse to give myself that permission. I can stop myself from losing it." By this time, I was aware that, ironically, my voice was pretty loud and I was speaking pretty quickly, as if to get as much into the eight minutes as possible.

"Well done. That realisation seems to be big for you."

"It's just...just that I have never thought of it like that at all."

"I am afraid we only have two minutes left so I would like to leave you with something to try. The beauty of it is that you don't have to wait for a situation where you might lose it. You could just as easily use it when you are participating in a meeting and thinking of what to say. But I have found it also works really well in the situations we have been talking about." He had been scribbling some notes which he now handed to me:

| Stimulus | S.T.O.P. | Response |

He continued. "We were taught at school that for every stimulus there is a response. So, in the circumstances we have been discussing, somebody says something and we respond angrily to that. Our angry response, as we now know, is because between the stimulus and response, there's another step: we choose to respond to the stimulus in that way. Incidentally, the more heated we feel after the stimulus, the more time we should put before our response – drag it out. But the question for me has always been: how, in the moments between stimulus and response, do I ensure I do the most effective thing? I have always felt there is a need to push pause, like on the TV remote, so that I can stop and think. And then I came across the acronym S.T.O.P, which I think does just that and I would be interested if it (and the rest of this model) works for you as well. S.T.O.P. stands for: 'Stop', which pushes the pause button nice and firmly; 'T' is for 'Think', like think of what I want to achieve, or what the objective of the conversation originally was, or what win-win I want to achieve, whatever is appropriate; 'O' is for 'Options', as in what are my options in this particular case, what are the different ways in which I might respond; and 'P' is for Proceed with the most appropriate or effective option or options, those that are likely to achieve my objective etc. Did you get all that?" he said looking at me scribbling furiously.
"Yeah, I think so. How's this?"

S	• Stop!
T	• Think
O	• Options
P	• Proceed

5

"That's it. And I guess that's it for now. Would you like to try out various applications of this model and discuss what you find next time?"

"Yes, I think that would be helpful. Thanks a lot for the session."

"Pleasure. And good luck with Linda."

"Thanks."

....

Linda was five minutes late for our meeting – a bad omen if ever there was one. In fact, I was just noting the time when she knocked and came in. "Sorry I am a little late, Tony, but I do have a reasonable explanation."

"Hi, Linda, come in."

"I have been trying to get in to see Dr Cohen all week and at last he was able to see me this morning. That's not all, though; he has put in a massive order on our monthly special. Seems like the hospital were not happy with their previous provider and so our timing was spot on. And there will be more monthly orders. Not only that, but my meeting with her meant that I am able to report back that I made all the calls I promised since our last meeting. I did it, Tony!"

"Well done, Linda," I responded, quite pleased deep down that I didn't need to use what I had learnt with Paulo. "I can hear the excitement in your voice, something I haven't heard since you had that record month just after I joined the company. Sit down."

"Thank you, Tony. Yes, you are right. I am excited. Things seem to be turning for me."

---

[5] Adapted from Timothy Gallwey: The Inner Game of Work (2000): 141-164

"Good. Tell me what you have been doing differently since we last met."

"Nothing earth-shattering – just the stuff we are supposed to do. I always used to avoid making the phone calls to set up the appointments but this week I did, and it seems to be working."

"Did anything change in the way you approached these calls?"

"I guess two things. I faced them head on. I made a list of the people I needed to call this week and called five every day. And, secondly, I did this first thing every morning. Normally I used to stretch my calls out all day – which meant that the pain of calling was stretched out all day too. And I never used to use a list because I know who I am supposed to be calling. But I got huge satisfaction from ticking them off the list as I contacted them. I remembered this is what I used to do when I was hitting my numbers. I know it is not everything – there are other parts of the sales process that we discussed last time that I also need to tighten up on – but it all starts with these calls. It's not as though I didn't know this: it's the way I did things when I consistently hit my targets. I don't know how I managed to get out of the habit. I guess it can happen over time..."

"It sure can," I said. "What can we do to ensure that this new approach becomes a new practice or habit for you, and that you don't drift back into your bad habits?"

"Well, what I have done is to block my diary out for half an hour every morning first thing. That's all it takes for me to get through the calls. And that way, it's not even painful."

"So you have blocked out your diary every morning for thirty minutes. Okay. Anything else?"

"No, that's about it, I think. Why? Have I missed something?"

"No, it could be as simple as that. Let's check. What might go wrong with this plan?"

"Well, when I need to go into theatre with the doctors it is often first thing in the morning. When this happens it will upset this new practice. Also, it's probably what happened to me when I fell out of this habit over time."

"Okay, so on the days when you go into theatre, what can you do to ensure this practice doesn't fall into disuse as it did previously?"

"I could move the thirty minute block to the first free time slot I have."

"So that would resolve similar problems you might have around meetings and other commitments?"

"Yes."

"Why did this practice fall into disuse last time and how can we prevent that from happening again?"

"I think it is just a matter of discipline, Tony. Previously, I just made a mental note that I was going to phone a certain number of doctors during the day – not during a specific period of the day. That was the first thing. The second was that I often hadn't considered who I would be calling."

"Are you saying, therefore, that if you are disciplined and specific about the time and who you are going to call, that this should work consistently for you?"

"Yes, provided it is not merely a mental exercise – I must write the time and the people into my diary."

"Good point. When do you intend to make these entries into your diary?"

"I thought I would spend ten to twenty minutes every morning planning, and this would include the process we are talking about."

"Okay. And what criteria will you use to ensure that you see the right people at the right time."

"I'm sorry, I am not sure what you mean."

"Well, how do you currently decide which customers to call?"

"It's a bit of thumb suck, really. I know who I haven't seen recently and so I will put their names down."

"What are the pros and cons of doing it this way?"

"I've never really considered it but I suppose planning is a good thing. Umm...but I suppose it is a bit hit and miss."

"'Hit and miss'?"

"Well, it's dependent on my memory, I suppose."

"And the downside of that is...?"

She smiled. "Well, I suppose I am like everyone else and might forget the odd name from time to time."

"And what would be the consequence of that?" I asked returning the smile.

"Well, I suppose it means that, at worst, in theory anyway, someone could fall off my calling 'list'."

"And at best?"

"I guess my calls will be infrequent and irregular."

"And what might that result in?"

"I guess it might affect my relationship with the customer at some level...oops, and I suppose it gives the opposition a huge opportunity."

"So, how might we remedy this? How can we create greater consistency in your calling process?"

"I think the first thing I probably need is to get my customer list from Accounts. Then at the beginning of each month – I suppose it might be any period, it could be yearly or quarterly for example - I could put the names down in the weeks or days I intend to call them." I could almost see her brain change gear. "Actually, I could plan for a year ahead and then review it quarterly, monthly and weekly in advance, to see that I am seeing everyone enough."

"Good. And how would you know what is enough? Are your customers all of equal importance?"

"No, I suppose not. Some give us more business than others and I suppose I should see those more than I see others that give me less business."

"Linda, I am afraid our time is coming to an end and, as far as I recall, we are both attending the presentation in a few minutes. Before we go, however, what has stood out for you in this session? What are the most important things that you have learnt or arrived at?"

She thought for a few moments and then, with clarity I hadn't noticed before, succinctly listed four take-aways she had picked up and, without my prompting, indicated what she was going to do with them. Things were progressing nicely. Oh, and I had been wrong! Maybe sustainability wasn't altogether a lost cause.

"Okay," I said in conclusion. "That's great. And our agreement is still in place for the next three weeks? Are you still committed to it?"

"Oh, yes," she retorted with almost indecent haste. "I'm firing on all cylinders at the moment. I feel more energised than I think I have ever been."

"That's good to hear, Linda. Would it help if we followed through on your thoughts of segmenting your customers according to revenue?"

She nodded as we both got up to go to the presentation.

8. "Meetings, Meetings, Bloody Meetings"

(With apologies to John Cleese)

"Gee, I see Linda seems to be shooting the lights out. Whatever you said to her, keep saying it!" Paulo laughed. "Would you like to fill me in on your sessions with her?"

We spent the next ten minutes catching Paulo up on my discussions with her.

"Wow, quite a turnaround, Tony, well done." Somehow I knew he couldn't leave it there and that there were a couple of questions coming that would embed the learning for me. Sure enough..."So, what are the three most important things you learnt about turning the performance of a team member around?"

I smiled. Somehow, once again, I was prepared for the question. You see, the beauty of these conversations with Paulo was that in a relatively short period of time I seemed, naturally, to ask myself the same questions he did. It was as if, somehow, I was automatically not only generating these questions for myself but also automatically self-correcting when I went off-beam. It wasn't that I was spending so much more time thinking of these things; rather, it seemed as though I was having the same old conversations I had in my head – and that I thought every manager had – but now they were proving far, far, more effective.

"Firstly," I replied, "don't delay difficult conversations. Secondly, be firm but fair. And, thirdly, ensure that they take responsibility for what they do and don't do – don't collect their monkeys."

"You've got that pretty clear in your mind," he said returning the smile. "Which one of those, for you, ensures that their performance will remain sustainable after the turnaround?"

Oops, I hadn't planned on that question but before I knew it, my answer was rolling off my tongue. "I think it's the third one. It's as if somewhere along the way it's the fact that they stop taking responsibility for their every action or lack of action that lands them in trouble. Sales people seem to have a whole armoury of excuses for everything they don't achieve. Once they have taken back that responsibility, I think my job becomes a matter of managing that responsibility."

"Okay, that's a really interesting perspective. What would you like to discuss today?"

"Everything seems to be going fine at the moment. The numbers are great for this time of year and there is plenty in the pipeline. I am having brief but focused conversations with each of my team members on a weekly basis and I think those conversations are playing no small part in the direction that the numbers are going. I think, though, that the area that I am not sure about is when I have our monthly team meetings. Often I wonder whether they serve any purpose at all. They just seem to be report back meetings."

"What is it about team meetings that you specifically want an answer to today?"

"Well, on the one hand, I am holding the weekly individual meetings and am covering what I need to cover, I think, with the individual sales people. On the other hand, the team has always had monthly meetings to discuss overall results and decide things like where we should be focusing. But I have already discussed each person's results with them and we have discussed where they should be focusing. The team meeting just seems like unnecessary repetition in some ways – although it is at a collective level. And I hate unnecessary meetings..."

"Okay, I'd like to delve a little deeper into your individual meetings before we look at the team meetings. What is your primary purpose of having the meetings with each team member each week?"

"I have never put my thoughts about this into words but I think each of these meetings is about the individual's performance and about their development. I try to help them find ways that they can do even better in their sales process so that their numbers exceed their targets and, in the process, develop them as sales people and, come to think of it, hopefully as people."

"That's interesting – and I would like to come back to that. So, when you are helping them with their performance, where is your focus – on the numbers, or how to get there?"

"No, thanks to you, we focus on all the critical variables in the process, the inputs and throughputs. I think that's been at the core of the team's success in exceeding targets this year."

"Good, I just wanted to clarify that. And your comment about developing them as sales people and people?"

"Yes, that has been interesting. I think it started with me having discussions with some of them about integrity where they may have felt under pressure to cross the line in order to make some sales or keep ahead of what the competition were offering their clients and prospects. Some of these evolved into discussions around the company's values and how they underpin every decision that we make. And then several went on to discuss or develop their own values. I always thought that stuff was esoteric but, gee, it has been really powerful for some of them. They just seem to be so much more assured of their decision-making and...and of themselves."

"That sounds great, Tony. I am glad you are prepared to explore areas outside your comfort and even belief zone. So, if your purpose for individual meetings is individual performance and development, what would your purpose for team meetings be?"

"As I said earlier, traditionally they have been report back meetings where I give them the monthly results but it seems such a waste of time to hold a meeting to do that. The guys are busy and don't need to waste time in meetings that don't add value."

"Surely results can't be unimportant?"

"It's not so much the results themselves, but the dreary routine of going through them."

"So, it may not be so much the 'what' as it might be the 'how'?"

"Yes, when you put it like that."

"Okay, is it okay if we come back to that? I would just like to go back and explore the purpose avenue." I smiled. Exploring always sounded like fun when it was initiated by Paulo – and inevitably was. "What should the purpose of your team meetings be? Is there anything worthwhile that you should be meeting about?"

"I can see you are turning my thinking on its head!" Now I grimaced. "I guess the meetings be for discussions we are unable to have effectively in the corridor. They should be about the most important issues as we see them in the moment. As far as the monthly results are concerned, they might be a gap analysis: How are we doing as a team against our targets? What progress are we making against our vision? That type of thing. What's the gap between our every activity and the big picture we want to reach?"

"Okay, good. Would it help if we then measure your current meetings against this purpose so that we can identify where they might be achieving the purpose and where they might be missing the purpose?" I nodded and he continued. "So, currently you feel that the report back meetings are a waste of time because they don't seem to add value. What specifically do you do in these meetings that you don't believe is aligned to their purpose?"

"Firstly, as I said, we share the monthly results of the team in respect of each of the product lines. (Later, I take up each person's individual contribution with them in our individual one on ones, so there is no need to do it here). And, secondly, we go through the previous month's minutes and check how they are each doing against their undertakings."

"Okay, let's take the first part. Why is that a waste of time, if measured against your purpose?"

"I just think there are more effective ways of using the time. The team results are circulated to each team member and if they analysed them prior to the meeting we wouldn't need to go through them for an hour."

"Are you saying that you go through them in the team meeting because you are concerned that otherwise they wouldn't analyse them?"

"I wasn't – but that's probably accurate, when I come to think about it."

"Does that mean you may have accepted one of their monkeys?"

"Walked into that one, didn't I. You are absolutely right!"

"What would a more effective approach look like?"

"I think I need to clarify my expectations and let them know that they need to have read...actually, analysed, the team results for each meeting."

"Otherwise? I mean, what would be the consequence for them?"

"Well, they wouldn't be able to participate meaningfully in the team discussions around how we are going to move forward and achieve the big picture as a team – what strategies and tactics we are going to put in place."

"And this is important, why?"

"Firstly, because they will be disempowering themselves because they won't have the knowledge to base any views on; and, secondly, it will take them some time to pick up how all this cascades down to their individual positions."

"And the impact of that?"

"Well, the impact of that is that they won't fully understand the parts of the big picture and they will therefore be limited in making decisions – and if they can't make the best decisions for their individual businesses, sooner or later their performance is likely to be affected."

"Alright. So you will circulate the monthly results by email and clarify your expectations of them to analyse those results and why. Where does this leave you as far as holding more effective team meetings? Do you actually need them?"

"I thought about that but think we do; especially now that you have got me to define the purpose of the meetings. The individual meetings are really good – they get us achieving at ground level. But I think it's important that each person has an understanding of how they fit into the bigger scheme of things – in fact, they often need to be reminded that they are part of a bigger cog. I think the team meetings achieve that. But now that I think of it, in the light of what we have been discussing, I think we can shorten the monthly meetings drastically. I inherited a team meeting that lasts four hours – that has always seemed ridiculous to me but we always seemed to fill the four hours. I guess that's what happens with meetings: they will swell to take up whatever time period you give them. So, maybe we should plan for meetings of an hour..."

"That's a big step down. Are you sure you will be able to achieve all you need to in that time?"

"Maybe, maybe not. We won't know until we try. Besides, now that we have defined the purpose, we can ensure that all items of the agenda are focused on taking us closer to achieving the purpose. Over time, we have just worked off the previous minutes and as I think of the current minutes in my head now, there's got to be a whole whack of stuff that actually doesn't fit there. So this is an opportunity to audit what we talk about and ensure that we focus only on agenda items that take us closer to achieving the purpose. Also, the minutes become like the monthly results – boring! We just report back as to who has done what they said they would do and who hasn't. All in all, the meeting is probably ten – maybe twenty on good days – percent discussion and the rest reporting back. And report backs can once again be done by email prior to the meeting. So, ideally, when meeting time comes everyone knows what has been done and what hasn't, and (more importantly) we are in a position to discuss whatever is most important to us at that moment. And, perhaps now and then, the discussion will need to be about why we as a team are falling short of our financial targets or why we are not taking responsibility for things in the minutes"

"I am glad you have been able to develop your thinking in this conversation. So, you will drop the current 'robotic minutes to minutes' approach and you have designed an agenda with items that take you closer to achieving the purpose. Is there anything you could do with the agenda design that might help the team focus more effectively on achieving the purpose?"

"Yeah, but firstly I think we could cut the meeting down to one hour. As for the agenda, I think it should have three items: is there anything important that we need to discuss in the results? Is there anything important that stands out from the minutes? (That can normally be done in five minutes, or maybe fifteen). And then the main event: What is the most important issue or challenge we have at the moment?"

"I notice that your agenda items are in the form of questions."

"Yes, I have always had a problem with agendas that contain bland general items...I prefer to try to change those items so that they might be more specific and more pertinent. In fact, when we have decided what?"

"More specific and pertinent?'

"Yes, I think I am saying that I would like them go to the root of what the discussion will be about...the root of the issue...In fact, when an item is raised in answer to the items on the agenda, perhaps we need to find the right question which specifically and pertinently defines the issue."

"That sounds interesting. What do you think that will achieve?"

"Well, I think it would get more attention from the team members for a start – they are more likely to start thinking about the issue as a result of being prompted by a question. I think they will find that a more interesting and...yes, to pick up on something I said earlier, a more empowering approach. Actually, all this suggests that they are likely to be more prepared for meetings – they will have applied their mind more to what is going on – and so conversations will be more considered and should therefore be shorter. Hey, I think this can work. It's worth a try."

"Okay, that was my next question – do you want to give it a try? I guess the question now is: how will you broach these changes with the team? How will you get their buy-in?"

"I suppose I could share my thoughts with them and see what they think?"

"What do you think they are likely to think?"

"I think they are also bored with the meetings. But the changes mean they need to take more responsibility – so maybe they will baulk at the changes."

"What kind of leader do you want to be?"

"Gee, where did that come from? What do you mean?"

"What do you think your authentic leadership style is?"

"Authentic? That's a big, big question. If you had asked me before I took this sales management role, I think I saw myself as a driven person with huge ambitions – the achievement of my goals was everything. Actually, I suppose that hasn't actually changed, now that I think of it. I am still driven. I still want to achieve. But something is different...I don't think I am as self-centred as I was then. The truth is we managers can't achieve the goals our teams are set without those very same teams contributing. So my lesson has been that I can only achieve my goals – the steep targets the organisation sets me – if I get the best out of my team members. And as strange as it would have sounded to me in my previous lifetime, I no longer believe that this is achieved by merely throwing money at the problem, by incentivising. It's got to be something deeper than that. Something that starts touching the...the...soul of my team members – gee, I don't think I have ever used the 's' word; at work or at home. I wonder where that came from. But somehow if I don't help them to improve their lives, themselves as people, I won't get their best. I am rambling but my thoughts seem to be coming together from somewhere – if I don't try to help them become the best people they can be, then can I expect them to produce their best? I don't know."

"I am hearing that your authentic leadership style has to do with helping the people you work with strive to become the best they can be. How would you ideally achieve that?"

"I think it's about being a role model and about working with them to achieve their objectives."-

"So, it's collaborative?"

"Yes, collaborative and facilitative. You have taught me that. What you are doing right now – helping me to learn by thinking more, and thinking more effectively."

"And tell me more about this role model thing..."

"Well, if I am wanting certain behaviour from my people, it's no good me displaying the opposite or conflicting behaviour. And if changes, especially in behaviour, need to be made, then my behaviour should also reflect the behaviour needed."

"Okay, so let's try this. What type of leadership style do your meetings reflect?"

"They've changed, I believe. In the beginning, I think I dominated the meetings I conducted. It was my way or the highway. Now, I concentrate on asking the right questions, the most important one in the moment – my job is to find it – and to listen to the discussion after that, involving as many viewpoints around the table as possible, so that I can find the next question. I think I speak far less now – probably about twenty percent of the time, if I can help it."

"Sounds collaborative and facilitative?"

"I guess you are right. Role modeling, right? Actually, come to think of it, our discussion earlier really helps. The notion of being aware of the purpose of the meetings really helps in raising the most important and relevant questions."

"And so how will you use this information to get the buy-in you want?"

"Well, what has just sunk in for me is that I want my meetings to reflect my leadership style – and that's collaborative and facilitative. But I am worried that it sounds a little unfocused – does it?"

"You were talking a little earlier about the extent to which you have always been goal-driven. Do you think your personality will ever allow you to be anything but collaborative, facilitative and focused?"

"No, I guess not. It has also just struck me that whilst I have come up with an alternative way to conduct more meaningful meetings; this is just my current view. Between them they are likely to be able to come up with something even more effective if I ask the right questions and generate the right level of conversation."

"Okay, so do you want to be consultative in your approach, or participative?"

"What do you mean?"

"What will the purpose of that meeting be?"

"For me to enable them to design more meaningful and effective team meetings."

"And how would you do that?"

"I would start by telling them the purpose of the meeting and asking them to rate the current meetings out of ten in terms of meaningfulness and effectiveness. That is likely to get things going! There are often complaints about their length and questions as to whether they really need to attend. So, once they have scored the meetings, this will lead to a lively discussion on why they scored them as they did. Once we have these reasons on the table, we can move onto how we might improve them. I think I will divide them into eight pairs for this and ask each pair to come up with the five most important ways, in order of importance, that they think we could make the meetings more meaningful and most effective."

"Before we get on to the mechanics of your process, may I just clarify with you: Whose decision is this going to be in the end? Yours or theirs?"

"Oh, theirs, definitely. Why?"

"When you help them come to an answer or decision, you are using a participative approach. Where you are bouncing something off them to see if they can persuade you away from a decision you have already made, that's a consultative approach."

"Thanks, that is an interesting distinction. Is one better than the other?"

"No, save that participative is more empowering than consultative. But there are times when consultative is good and times when participative is good. Many good leaders will vacillate between them. And both fall within your parameters of being collaborative and facilitative. Personally, I prefer to err on the empowering side, the participative approach – that suits my personality and leadership style more, I think. The really big mistake, however, is to use language that suggests you are being participative when in fact you have already made up your mind and are actually being consultative. Next time you approach them, don't be surprised if they hold back – I mean normally they don't like getting caught out twice. But if you are honest with them, that's a different matter."

"Thanks again, that's good stuff."

"Okay, where were we. Oh, yes, why did you pick 'five'?"

"Well, I was going to say three but I thought that might not stretch them and we might have the same things on the table from each pair – we would lose out on some creativity. So if we stretched ourselves we might come up with different stuff rather than more of the same. Actually, I know, I will ask them to brainstorm ten ways and give them two minutes to do them in. That will mean each pair will have some time pressure too and if I impress on them not to think too hard on each one and to merely see what comes up for them, we might get some stuff that's off the wall."

"Okay, so now you will be sitting with more than a hundred options, give or take some overlaps. What will you do with that?"

"Well, I would ask each pair to prioritise them and to discuss just why each one is important to them. They would need to decide in doing so which of their options are not negotiable. There are eight pairs altogether so I would then get pairs of pairs to debate their list with each other – debate them robustly – to come out with the best ten between them, in order of importance. And then we would repeat that four against four and see what we come out with. And then eight against eight. Might be fun. The team as a whole could then decide whether any of the options that may have fallen off the table in the process, should be brought back and what the action plan is going to be to put all of this into practice."

"Sounds an interesting approach. It will certainly get some friendly competitiveness going. Sounds worth trying. Let me know what happens. Listen, I have something else I need to discuss with you before we end but first, are you okay with that process – anything that concerns you or you are not sure about?"

"No, I think I am okay with it. What do you want to talk about?"

"Well, I wondered whether you felt ready to pick up some new challenges. This is highly confidential but I have been asked to take over Ntombi's position when she retires at the end of the financial year and your team has shot the lights out in the relatively short time you have been in your position. You are a quick learner, but what we've been really pleased with is the way in which you get the best out of your people. So, we were wondering whether you would consider..."

Ten minutes later I walked out of Paulo's office with a distinct bounce in my step – a bounce not unlike the one I had when I walked into the office on my first day as a Sales Manager, not too many months earlier. But there was a difference: I was different, very different. I had learnt so much about myself, about people and about business. Unlike that first day, I had learnt that the more you know, the more you know there is to know. I knew that my journey had just started in relative terms and who knows where this journey will still take me.

As I write this, I can hear Paulo's voice in my head, asking: "What is the most important thing that you learnt as a Sales Manager?" I guess my answer is...

> When I truly help my people to start becoming the best they can be, I start becoming the best I can be!

Bibliography

Buys, L. 2007. *Management by Coaching – 7 Basic Keys.* Knowres

Buys, L. 2010. *High-Performance Coaching for Managers – 7 Effective Keys.* Knowres

Downey, M.2003. *The Effective Coach.* Texere

Gallwey, WT. 1975. *The Inner Game of Tennis.* Jonathan Cape Ltd

Gallwey, WT. 2000. *The Inner Game of Work.* Random House

Goleman, D.1999. *Working with emotional intelligence.* Bloomsbury

Goleman, D, Boyatsis, R & McKee, A. 2002. *The new leaders: transforming the art of leadership into the science of results.* Little, Brown

Rock, D. 2006. *Quiet Leadership.* Harper Collins

Rosen, K. 2008. *Coaching Salespeople into Sales Champions.* John Wiley & Sons

Strachan, D. 2007. *Making Questions Work.* Jossey-Bass

www.ingramcontent.com/pod-product-compliance
Lightning Source LLC
Chambersburg PA
CBHW071239170526
45165CB00003B/1169